# RIO GRANDE

The People and Politics of One of America's Greatest Rivers

Text and Photography
by Mike Leggett

LONGSTREET PRESS
Atlanta, Georgia

Published by
LONGSTREET PRESS, INC.
A subsidiary of Cox Newspapers,
A division of Cox Enterprises, Inc.
2140 Newmarket Parkway
Suite 118
Marietta, GA  30067

Printed in the United States of America

1st printing 1994

Library of Congress Catalog Card Number: 93-81146

ISBN 1-56352-139-3

This book was printed by Horowitz/Rae, Cedar Grove, N.J.

Book Design and Production by Graham and Company Graphics, Inc., Atlanta, Georgia.

Color Separations by Holland Graphics Inc., Mableton, Georgia

*Cover photograph: The mouth of Boquillas Canyon in Big Bend National Park.*

To my Dad
(1919–1994)

To my wife, Rana, and
Casey, Laurie and Dan

A BROWN PELICAN,
ONCE AN ENDANGERED
SPECIES, FLIES OVER
THE SURF AT THE
MOUTH OF THE RIVER.
THE END OF THE LINE.

# TABLE *of* CONTENTS

Silverton
Creede
Rio Grande
25
Santa Fe
Albuquerque
40
Rio Grande
RIO GRANDE
Las Cruces
El Paso
Juarez
20
10
Austin
Rio Grande
Big Bend
National
Park
35
10
San
Antonio
Nuevo
Laredo
Laredo
Rio Grande
Brownsville
Matamoros

*Staff of the Austin American-Statesman*

# RIO GRANDE

THE RIO GRANDE DOESN'T
LOOK MUCH LIKE A
RIVER HERE AT STONY
PASS, BUT THIS IS THE
BEGINNING OF THE
WHOLE THING. MELTING
ICE TRICKLES DOWN
FROM 14,000 FEET TO
TRAVEL NEARLY 2,000
MILES TO THE GULF OF
MEXICO.

# THE BEGINNING

I often tell people that I live in Austin, when in reality I live about 60 miles away in the little country town of Burnet.

Though it's named for the first governor of Texas, few people know where Burnet is. They confuse it with Boerne to the south or pronounce it Bur-*net* instead of *Bur*-net, as in Burnet, durnit! They can recognize the state capital, though, and rather than confuse them, I'll just say Austin, I'm from Austin.

That's a geographical generalization I can live with, though I'd rather not; but it is sort of how I originally came to spend an entire September traveling the Rio Grande and eventually to write this book. Maybe the best way to explain it is with an old Dean Martin movie from many years back—*Four for Texas*, I think— that kind of condensed Hollywood ignorance about the Lone Star State, geography and basically all things good and natural.

In this movie, Dean and a couple of his pals ride out from Galveston on their horses. They leave what should be the marshes and swamps of nineteenth-century Galveston and ride west, right into a landscape of cactus, mountains and rocks. No alligators, mosquitoes or Karankahua Indians, just west Texas desert. It was comical in a way, but damned irritating to any real Texans. However, being chauvinistic about Texas isn't necessarily a defense against ignorance. Nothing prepared me, for instance, for having to face just how dumb, how blissfully, arrogantly ignorant I was about Texas' most famous river, the Rio Grande.

I became painfully aware, during a month-long trip from the river's beginning to its end, just how my own views and others' had been shaped by Hollywood, by a few trips across the river in south Texas and even by stories about wetbacks and bad jokes about Boys Town.

There wasn't really a plan to spend a month on the river, just a few days looking at some of the environmental issues that Texas and Mexico are grappling with at the end of the twentieth century. But then I looked at a map and there was the Rio Grande

## DAY ONE

*Leaving Texas is a sweet and sour experience. Early morning up through central Texas was nice because there were deer to look at and sights to see, but then I had to face the fact that I was leaving behind dove season and still had to drive through the Panhandle during the day. Frankly, it's anesthetizing, but the only way to go. 580 miles to the border with New Mexico, but I make it into Colorado by 6:30. Thinking about the Rio Grande has me checking out other rivers I cross on the way up. I have checked out a company vehicle, but the damn thing only holds 10 gallons of gas. I have to keep stopping every little while to fill up. Heavy thunderstorms kill my plan to camp for the night. I turn on the radio and drive until I get to Alamosa. 12 miles a gallon in this piece of junk. Fast-food chicken makes me sick and I spend the night with diarrhea.*

running clean back up through New Mexico, into Colorado and well back up into the mountains above Silverton.

I'd been there, without really thinking about it and without connecting that sluice of fast, cold Colorado water with the slow, muddy trickle at El Paso or the gin-clear ocean of Lake Amistad. How could I write about the Rio Grande, about any of the social and environmental swirls of life on the river, without seeing and being on the whole river?

The genesis for this series began there. I loaded up a four-wheel drive vehicle with a tent and sleeping bag, some diet drinks, jerky and trail mix, my fly rod and a gasoline credit card and hit the road, with no real concept of what I would find, or even what needed to be found. Most nights I slept on the ground, without the tent. I came to take pride in being able to sleep better on rocky ground than in a motel room.

There were nights spent lonely and confused, missing my family and wondering what the hell I had gotten myself into. Daytimes I drove, stopping where I could to touch the river and talk with people about it. I tended to drive in spurts, talking to myself or listening to whatever talk radio I could find. I learned that G. Gordon Liddy has a radio show and that the deep canyons of the upper Rio Grande are the only places on earth you can't get Rush Limbaugh.

The trip itself represents a microcosm of the Rio Grande. I left stifling, 100-degree heat in Texas and 1,000 miles later was standing beneath a snow bank 50 miles above Creede, Colorado. That pile of dirty snow, atop 14,000-foot Stony Pass, spits the first water into the river. The Rio Grande at Stony Pass is literally nothing more than a trickle, but other rivers and creeks add their share and pretty soon you have a river. Instead of the hot, dry desert air of south Texas, there's very little oxygen up there, and I huffed and puffed around, exploring and taking pictures.

We start at an abandoned gold mine and end in the salt waters of the Laguna Madre nearly 2,000 miles away. I loved the overlapping of cultures I found on the Rio Grande maybe more than anything else. Storing away some of the history and especially the geography became a part of every day I spent on the river. I've been back twice more since that first trip. As the river passes through Colorado and New Mexico and finally back into the deserts of Mexico and Texas, the Rio Grande really only gets deep in the man-made reservoirs, but it changes faces many times.

To the descendants of early European settlers in southern

Colorado, it's one river; to the Native Americans who first lived in the San Luis Valley where it begins, it's another. Later Indians, the Pueblos and Navajos, picked up the river in New Mexico and used it, as did their ancient and mysterious predecessors, the Anasazi.

Texans, Mexicans, New Mexicans, all see the river in different ways. It can be a border and an agricultural water source in Texas, a laundry and shower on the Mexican side. The Rio Grande has been dammed up, pumped dry and filled with sewage. It has been diverted, channelized and bridged. But still it goes on.

I drove more than 4,500 miles up and down the Rio Grande on my round trip back to central Texas. I gained new respect for the early tamers of the West, the men and women brave enough to cross the river in search of God knows what, for the Native Americans who already lived there and for the animals that hang on still.

However, only dismay could describe what has been done to the river in the name of progress and how little is being done to protect it. The Rio Grande already has been designated one of the top 10 endangered rivers in the United States, a rather meaningless status without a first-hand view.

That's what this book is intended to be, one traveler's view of the river and some of the people who treasure it, depend on it and live alongside it. Others have chronicled the history of the Rio Grande, the battles and treaties, as well as the lives of many of the people. What you'll find here is just the spewing out of one quick, rattling bounce through a storied part of the American West. ■

# LOST TRAIL

STONY PASS, COLO. — I was lost and needed direction, and talking with somebody would get rid of that feeling that the world had been raptured while I drove. I needed to know there were still other humans up here in the mountains. The gate to Lost Trail Ranch was closed but a sign invited visitors inside. I went.

A 200-yard dirt track ran to the headquarters cabin, where it ended in a swarm of dogs—barking, jumping, squealing dogs that came pouring in a hairy stream through a hole cut right through the cabin's front door. Out of the haze of hounds, a white-haired woman appeared on the front porch. It was a magician's trick rendered no less startling by the fact that it was no trick at all. The clattering dogs draw attention to themselves, and their human companion steps outside, through the door in the normal way. But it's a nice touch.

The woman—gray-haired, a little heavy, could be 50, could be 70—introduces herself as Carol Ann Getz. "That's Carol Ann Wetherill Getz," she says, waiting for the name to strike a chord, which it does. "My grandfather was Clayton Wetherill. He discovered Mesa Verde. I use my maiden name because it opens doors for me around here." Any Colorado native and most visitors recognize the name from Wetherill Mesa, one area of Mesa Verde, America's best-known ancient Indian ruin. Getz rattles off the books written about members of her family; she is even working on one herself.

Stacks of books and papers decorate the room, witness to Getz's quiet lifestyle and affinity for history. Through the window by the fireplace, out past the homemade, wood-burning hot tub, the pasture slopes away toward the rushing waters of the Rio Grande. Here the river is narrow, clear, loud. It is the Rio Grande of today still wearing its old, never-go-out-of-style suit.

Getz has lived at Lost Trail Ranch for nearly 60 years, since her father bought the 640 acres for $1,500. Lost Trail is the last deeded land on the Rio Grande, upstream from the fish hatchery her grandfather ran when he wasn't exploring the mountains and deserts of

## DAY TWO

*Absolutely beautiful day in Alamosa. It's cool enough for a sweat suit, but I run down to the river and watch huge carp rolling in the brownish water. Probably stained by agricultural runoff, because it's clear above and below here. Taking off for the head of the river. I got directions from a nice woman on how to find the beginnings of the river, but have to wait for morning to make the drive. I am 30 miles from a phone and can't call Casey on her 14th birthday. Decided to camp where I saw an elk cow and calf cross in front of me. Too lonely to build a fire. Ate jerky and trail mix for supper. Pitched the tent, which was broken from son Dan's last camping trip. It smelled of cat urine. Air mattress went flat. Slept on the ground, listening to coyotes.*

the Four Corners. Lost Trail Ranch once was a working cattle ranch, Getz said, but now offers llama pack trips into the wilderness along the upper Rio Grande. "There are more people now than before World War II, but not much else has changed," Getz says. "Before the war, when we'd see a car, we'd watch and hope they were coming to see us. Sometimes they were because the road ended here."

It still does in its own way, changing from a reasonably comfortable gravel road to a torture master's idea of fun just above Getz's ranch. From there, a traveler hoping to see the Rio Grande at its source must do battle with 15 miles of four-wheel-drive rock and mud to reach Stony Pass and the beginning of the river. "You can't make it up there this late in the day," Getz told me shortly after I arrived at Lost Trail. "I'll show you where to camp tonight and then you can go up in the morning. When you come back down we can visit."

We spent the rest of the afternoon with Getz posing for photos and taking me on a short hike around the ranch and down to the river. "But only if my friends can be in the pictures, too," she said, nuzzling and baby talking the mass of dogs. Turned out the pooches are mostly strays, picked up off the nearby county road and nursed and fed by Getz and her children. They have that way dogs do of adapting to new circumstances, reaching out with new love and companionship to whichever human is lucky enough to be standing in the right place. A robust 62-year-old, Getz lives on the Lost Trail Ranch until the first of October, when bad weather forces her down to winter quarters in Monte Vista. In the spring, she can't wait to get back to the only real home she's ever known. "I guess it just means peace to me," she said. "When we go back, we have what we call re-entry syndrome, the phones and traffic. Some people get scared up here. It's a chosen way of life. We're competent and we've got horse sense."

This far up the Rio Grande, Getz has never had to worry about the politics of the river. There's no flap about endangered species. NAFTA is something on television. Water rights never come up. Urban stress is as unimaginable to her. Crime just doesn't exist. "[Life on the river] has always been just total freedom," Getz says. "You have to work, but that consists of being on pack trips, feeding stock, etc. It is kind of an illusion because the rest of the world doesn't live that way. The hard part is learning to live in the other world."

Getz seems oblivious to the fact that outside the close-knit area of Colorado she calls home, her grandfather isn't considered a hero by everyone. Many newcomers to the mountains blame him and his

CAROL ANN WETHERILL
GETZ CAN SIT IN HER
LIVING ROOM AND
LOOK OUT OVER THE
LAND HER FAMILY
HOMESTEADED WHEN
SHE WAS A CHILD.
THE LOST TRAIL RANCH
IS THE LAST PRIVATE
LAND ON THE UPPER
REACHES OF THE
RIO GRANDE.

THIS FROZEN STRETCH OF THE
RIO GRANDE RUNS THROUGH
CREEDE, COLO., A REMNANT OF
THE ROUGH AND TUMBLE MINING
DAYS OF THE EARLY TWENTIETH
CENTURY. BECAUSE THE TOWN
HAD NO SEWER SYSTEM,
RESIDENTS BUILT OUTHOUSES
OUT OVER THE RIVER, HENCE
THE NAME, "SHIT CRIK."

brothers for opening up what they consider to be sacred Native American land, but Getz sees him strictly in the role of pioneer and grand survivor. "I didn't know him because he died before I was born," she says. "The Wetherills came from Missouri and lived in Bluff, Utah." Clayton's father was an Indian agent appointed by President Ulysses S. Grant. The Utes of southwestern Colorado allowed the family to run cattle on tribal lands. It was on a swing through looking for strays one day that Clayton found Mesa Verde, the famed Cliff Palace and Spruce House.

After that, Clayton Wetherill tended his hatchery in winter and guided visitors into the desert and mountains in spring and summer. Getz is convinced that the extremes of desert life are what claimed his life at an early age. But Wetherills weren't the only settlers in the Upper Rio Grande Valley. Getz takes visitors to sites of long-destroyed cabins and cattle operations, mines and wells. Pieces of broken pottery dot the dirt road that runs through those areas. "That's how you can tell a family lived here," Getz says. "The women brought pottery, but when it was just men they used cans or pots or whatever for cooking."

During tours of the old home sites, Getz, as always surrounded by her pack of dogs, stoops to pick up square, rusty nails, remnants of barns and houses, before shooing me off on the rough, four-hour drive to the top of the river. Getz is waiting on the porch when I return, the ubiquitous dogs sprawled here and there in the sunshine. We visit for a few minutes, during which Getz throws out the names of half a dozen books she believes must be read to fully soak in the flavor of the river.

But that's a dish better served by her. "The river hasn't changed at all," Getz says. "There are changes but there aren't. The mountains haven't changed. Physically, it's timeless." But people have changed the river. "It's hard for me to imagine what has happened to the river down below. It makes me want to cry. I've never seen it all and I may never," Getz says. "We can go out here and drink this water. Down there, you don't dare wade in it. The river didn't do that, people did that."

People have changed other things as well in the forests around Getz's home. "This place has gone from trappers and Indians, to prospectors to cattlemen and now tourists," Getz says. "But the river and the mountains, they're always there. They're friendly to me. The history is interesting and intriguing to me, but we all die and the mountains and the river stay." ∎

## DAY THREE

Another great weather day. Carol Ann Getz shows me around the valley and points me to the head of the river. The road is a miserable, bumpy trail up through the mountains, but I made it to the snow bank and the official start of the trip around lunchtime. I hiked around and took some photos, ate cheese and crackers and peed in the river to see if I could beat it back to the Gulf. Perverse, but the situation called for it. I visited with some hunters and saw trout in the clear waters of the river. Hard not to be hunting up here. I've already seen some elk and deer. Finally found a pay phone and called home. Rana said she's thinking about selling the house, so I asked her to leave a forwarding address. There was a marijuana plant growing under the stairs leading to the second floor of the country store where I stopped. Found a nice little cabin with a fireplace to spend the night, but I miss Rana and Casey. Not sleeping well.

# LAST OF THE GRIZZLIES

GRIZZLY BEARS
LIVED ALONG
THE RIO GRANDE
NOT SO LONG
AGO. IN 1947,
CAROL ANN
GETZ'S FATHER
FOUND THIS
BRUTE OF A
BEAR TRAP
WITH A GRIZZLY
BEAR'S PAW
STILL HANGING
IN THE TEETH.
NOT MANY
YEARS LATER,
MONTE VISTA
RESIDENT ERNIE
WILKINSON
TRAPPED THE
LAST GRIZZLY
FROM THE RIO
GRANDE
DRAINAGE.

MONTE VISTA, COLO. — I like bears. You could say I love bears, I guess. Nothing would make me happier than to see bears, grizzlies especially, roaming again through the hills of the lower Rocky Mountains that once were their home.

But will they? Likely not. At least as long as people are out there. And I'm not talking about savage, red-eyed hunters slavering over bear carcasses shot full of holes with outsized long guns. I'm talking about touristy people, summertime residents, campers and mountain bikers. Those are the humans not prepared to deal with bears. Even cattle and sheep growers, generally unenthusiastic bear advocates, know how to cope with bears that trouble them.

It's the occasional bear-country person who doesn't even realize that by his very presence he's keeping bears relegated to a historical footnote. A grizzly bear expert in Montana said something to me once that stuck. Paraphrased it reads this way: It's not that bears can't tolerate people. It's the other way around. A grizzly bear could live real well in the alleys in New York City, but the people wouldn't tolerate it. Grizzly bears are our subject here, of course, since black bears are stable and even expanding in most ranges. That's due to the black bear's shy nature and the fact that they don't go in much for whacking the neighbor's prize bulls. Grizzly bears are different critters, though. Still mostly vegetarian and carrion eating, the grizzly is nonetheless blessed with a remarkable sense of himself and his place in nature, namely that he's the baddest S.O.B. out there. If it's the bull he wants, it's the bull he takes.

Ernie Wilkinson of Monte Vista knows about grizzly bears. He's an old-timer in the Rio Grande country, a taxidermist, hunter, guide and former bear man. Carol Ann Getz suggested I talk with him after she saw my fascination with an ancient bear trap that hangs in her family cabin on Lost Trail Ranch. The shark's tooth look of the trap jaws is made even more bizarre by what they hold: a grizzly bear's paw, gold hair still intact, with claws on one end and stripped foot bones on the other. Carol Ann's father found the trap on the mountain above the cabin in 1947. Back in those days, the grizzlies were hanging on in the face of stockmen who wanted them out of the valleys along the upper Rio Grande. The bears were still there, but living in their last days. The end was five years away.

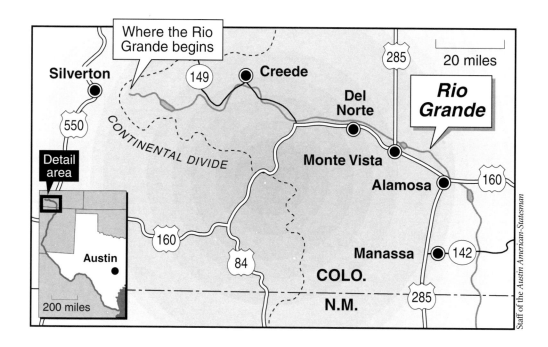

"I took a grizzly that was killing sheep up in Starvation Gulch on the south side of the Rio Grande," said Ernie Wilkinson. "That was 1952 and I was working as a government trapper, trapping coyotes and bear, whatever were bothering the animals." Wilkinson, 69, spent eight years in his trapper's job, learning the mountains well enough to now spend his time teaching mountain and winter survival classes. "I had a camp up in there and people would leave me notes about animals that were bothering stock," he said.

After each two-week round of his trapping area, Wilkinson would return to camp to check his next list of appointments. In 1952, he had a report of a bear attacking and killing sheep far up the river. "I did not know that this was a grizzly," Wilkinson said. There were no tracks in the rocky ground, but it wouldn't have mattered. "At that time, a bear was a bear," said Wilkinson in that slightly nasal mountain twang. "It was a fairly young bear, so there was probably some older ones up in there, too."

Wilkinson set his trap in the bear's killing range and soon had caught the smallish bear. "That was the only one that ever showed up," he said. "I never saw any others." And it would be the last reported grizzly in southern Colorado for 26 years, when an old sow was killed on the Brazos River. But stories persist about grizzlies having found their way back into the upper Rio Grande basin. Could the bears have returned? "I couldn't say that there is, I couldn't say that there isn't," Wilkinson said. "We're hearing all kinds of things down here about that." If they have, it will be to a much different world. Many of the sheep operations that summered near the head of the Rio Grande have gone the way of those earlier bears. Modern houses have sprouted up along the river itself. Summer houses sport flagpoles with banners signifying in which state the owner spends the rest of his life. I doubt that many of them give much thought to bears, especially to grizzly bears.

But I can't travel through bear country (it's still bear country, even if there are no bears) without viewing a nice piece of Rio Grande frontage and thinking: "I bet a bear killed an elk calf and ate it right there by those rocks." He could eat there again, too, but it wouldn't be an elk this time. I think much of my fascination with grizzly bears has to do with the fact that they can eat us, too, if they so choose.

I've slept on the ground in grizzly country in Alaska and Montana and Wyoming. Right there with me in that sleeping bag was always a prickly, palpable sense of vulnerability. I could stick a gun in with me, but that really only gave me a better chance of shooting myself or someone else in the dark. If the grizzly wanted me, he could have me and if I'm camped out there in his backyard—sort of a human tamale—then isn't that the way it should be. I wouldn't go willingly, but then neither would justice be served by blaming the bear.

He was there first. ■

# BOOTLEGGERS I HAVE KNOWN

SHORTY
WHEELER
REMEMBERS
THE RIO GRANDE
NOT FOR THE
WATER BUT FOR
THE ICE HE ONCE
CUT FROM THE
RIVER TO SELL
TO FARMERS IN
THE SAN LUIS
VALLEY, THE
LAND OF COOL
SUNSHINE. HE
ALSO KNEW
WHERE TO FIND
THE BEST
BOOTLEGGERS
WHO ONCE PLIED
THEIR TRADE IN
THE HILLS ALONG
THE RIVER.

SOUTH FORK, COLO. — I stopped for gas and jerky at a small grocery store that fronts a cluster of log cabins a few hundred yards from the Rio Grande.

The owner, assuming by my cowboy hat and jeans I was hunting or fishing, asked if I was having any luck. I explained my mission of traveling the river, talking with people and experiencing some of its history. "Then you've got to talk to Shorty," she said and picked up the phone. Just that quickly an interview was arranged at Shorty's home in Del Norte, 30 miles down the road.

A few hours later I'm sitting across a table from the man everybody calls Shorty, even though the grade school appellation doesn't fit any longer. No one is talking and the stress is starting to get to Shorty Wheeler. Sitting at the kitchen table of the manager's apartment in the retirement home he runs in the small, southern Colorado town, Wheeler is noticeably uncomfortable. He doesn't know what to say and for a talker's talker, that's a strain.

Wheeler, 80, is willing. He just doesn't know what I want to hear. I don't want to smother his thoughts with some expectation of my own and it's a standoff. His wife goes out for a walk. We stare at each other. I'm starting to get a bad feeling about it, but we're here, so I ask about his childhood around Del Norte. Anything that has to do with the river. Wheeler begins by telling stories about his childhood around Del Norte, about living with his grandparents and driving a school bus while he was in high school.

"God, I got $20 a month for that," he said, still searching for the right story about life in the San Luis Valley in the early 1900s. "I could take a girl to the picture show and get a sandwich and still have a nickel left from a dollar." Wheeler says he hunted and fished some in those days. "At that time, we could go out and kill 20 ducks at any time. You were in trouble for deer and there were no elk."

Wheeler said in about 1928 he drove up the Valley to watch game officials unload five train carloads of elk from Wyoming and Montana to begin rebuilding the Valley's herd from scratch. "That's the first elk I ever saw," he said. "I knew a man who said he killed the last 16 head of elk in Creede in 1916 to sell for meat."

Shorty searches again for the right tale of life along the Rio Grande, including one story about dealing with the lack of electricity when he was a young man. "In the wintertime, there would be enough cold weather to freeze the river two to three feet deep in the holes," he said. "I had the job of cutting the ice out of the river. We took it to Del Norte to keep the vegetables cold that they raised." Farmers used the ice to refrigerate produce grown in the fertile San Luis Valley, which still gets its irrigation water out of the Rio Grande. Shorty, the first Ice Man.

Shorty was in the restaurant business, too. Thirty-five years. He saw the comings of the Texans, who invaded the Valley to hunt, fish and buy land. He saw the arrival of Prohibition, he says, and his eyes light up. His wife leaves the room again and Wheeler leans across the table and begins to lay out the Valley nightlife scene, circa 1930. "From Prohibition to the 1930s, there was nothing but bootleggers in the Valley," Wheeler said. "Creede had the most and the best bootleggers, Del Norte was second. Just outside Monte Vista, there was a place called Lariat that had all Mexican bootleggers.

"Creede. If you wanted to fight, that was the place to go. They had big dances up there," he says, cackling at the thought. "Are you kidding? Every time I could get away I went up there. Took my wife sometimes before we were married.

"The bootleggers made their own whiskey," Wheeler said. "You'd go to their house to buy it, but the stills were back up in the hills. There's still old copper pipe and barrel staves at those places." One has to wonder about the quality of the whiskey, whether or not it was even more dangerous than the hard living forced on Valley residents by weather and geography. "We didn't know any different, so it was the best," Wheeler says. "It cost $1 a pint. I was about 17 years old then, but I ran around with some fellows that were older that I was. Besides, if you had the money, it didn't matter to the bootleggers."

Most people knew and tolerated the bootleggers, but every now and then the brewers had to contend with those damned

TEXAN CRAIG TINSLEY COMES TO SOUTHERN COLORADO TO FISH FOR RAINBOW TROUT IN THE RIO GRANDE. THE RIVER IN THIS PART OF ITS RUN IS ONE OF THE BEST FISHING STREAMS IN THE LOWER ROCKY MOUNTAINS.

revenuers, Wheeler said. "There was one fellow, owned a restaurant in Del Norte, who was a bootlegger, too. He got trapped at his still once by police officers and federal agents. The man just went out of that valley," Wheeler says. "He left his restaurant and still and was never heard from again."

Creede, 50 miles from the head of the river, was a mining town in those days, a rough and dangerous place to make a living or even hang out. Jack Dempsey learned to fight amongst the miners of the time. Shorty remembers, too, the primitive conditions that existed there. "They didn't have any plumbing or running water. So they built outhouses out over that creek that runs into the river right there in Creede. There were so many of them that people called it "Shit Crik," giving creek the mountain pronunciation that always brings chills to my spine."

It was the first hint I was given that the people of the upper reaches hadn't always been kind and reverent toward the Rio Grande. Time has worn away the Shit Crik label, but not always the attitude. I wouldn't have to go much farther down the river to find out how little things have changed. ◼

JUST ABOVE
SOUTH FORK,
COLO., THE RIO
GRANDE IS A
CLEAN, PRISTINE
TROUT STREAM,
NOTHING LIKE THE
MUDDY BORDER
RIVER OF MOVIES
AND LEGEND.

SACRED HEART
CATHOLIC CHURCH IN
DOWNTOWN ALAMOSA,
COLO., HAS BEEN IN
EXISTENCE FOR MORE
THAN 100 YEARS. IT IS
ONE OF THE MAINSTAYS
OF LIFE IN THE SAN
LUIS VALLEY.

# SACRED HEART CATHOLIC CHURCH

I'm a preacher's kid, born to the traditions—and prejudices—of the Southern Baptist Convention. No number of miles, cases of beer or dalliances with other churches can change my bloodline or banish certain things from my life.

I like loud, up-tempo music, male gospel groups with over-the-top tenors, and church members who aren't afraid to say "hidy" and offer to sign you up for something. It's a way of life I'm now able to view with more compassion and tenderness than I could 30 years ago when most of what I knew was that Wednesday night prayer meetings were screwing up my social life. Since then, I've agonized over my own definitions of God, religion and faith, a form of spiritual belly-button watching that carried me too far from the fun of being a Baptist. And the humor. When I visited Sacred Heart Catholic Church again, I got to see some of my Baptist upbringing in action and laugh a good laugh at the same time.

Back in the summer of 1987, my family and I had car trouble in southern Colorado. The rear wheel fell off our Suburban. We holed up at the Holiday Inn in Alamosa and spent our time playing whiffle ball at the local city park, visiting Great Sand Dunes National Park and going to Mass at the city's Catholic church, then celebrating its 100th anniversary. That's how my nephew Adam came to attend his first, and probably only, formal Mass.

My wife and I were then considering embracing Catholicism, though we'd later pass because of all the hoops they wanted us to jump through to justify having been divorced. But we were enthralled at the Mass conducted by Father Jim King, a bearded priest who sang his part in a breathtaking, elegant baritone voice.

At the proper point in the Mass, Father Jim, in the tradition of the Last Supper, says, "Peace be with you," and the congregation answers, "and with you." Then, again in keeping with tradition, Father Jim instructs the congregation to offer each other the sign of peace, usually a handshake or discreet hug and whisperings of

"Peace be with you." Adam, 12, the grandson of a Baptist minister and son of regular churchgoers, came to the church well steeped in the Protestant recruiting ethic. He viewed the goings-on and reacted in perfect Baptist style: hearty, shoulder-wrenching handshakes all around and loud declarations of "Hi! I'm Adam Leggett. Nice to meet you."

Sacred Heart parishioners, many of whom didn't even speak English, shook back but with bewildered looks on their faces. Our kids, on the other hand, were rolling on the floor. It was the highlight of the trip. Father Jim doesn't remember that incident, but if he did it would be with a laugh.

It takes a quiet sense of humor and strong sense of purpose to serve as the parish priest at Sacred Heart Catholic Church. In these days of an aging Catholic priesthood and in a San Luis Valley dominated politically by the Mormon church, Father Jim, 47, hangs on. And he does so with dignity and style.

It was his Mass six years ago that brought me back to the church again. My family and I were dumbstruck by the beauty of the service. It and the words of Huckleberry Finn define the edges of religion for me. Huck said of hogs under a church floor, encountered during his time spent with the Grangerfords after his raft was struck by a river boat, something to the effect that "most people go to church only when they have to but a hog is different."

In the east Texas churches where I grew up, there weren't hogs, but there was a fervor about being a Baptist and all it meant, especially the music. King could have been a gospel singing star there. I was fascinated by the bearded priest and wanted to know more about him and his church, about his singing voice. "I like to sing, so I do it," Father Jim says. "The celebration of Mass is a very personal thing to the priest and the congregation. You express yourself in that celebration. A priest who doesn't do that is in danger of just saying a Mass."

It's hard to imagine that as a problem at Sacred Heart, which exudes history and remains one of the building blocks of the community. The 75-year-old "new" building is thick adobe, has no air conditioning and is decidedly Southwestern in flavor.

Father Jim started coming to Colorado as a college student to work in the summers at a camp run by the Catholic church. Once he became a seminarian, moving back to the area just seemed natural. "I find generally I like any place I've been, but I like Sacred Heart most of all. It has a much more southwest-Hispanic feeling to the parish," he said. Masses are conducted in English and Spanish to accommodate the 20 percent of the parish which is completely Spanish speaking. There is a large (250 families) Guatemalan contingent, as well.

"This was an area on the Rio Grande that was rich with cottonwood trees," Father Jim said. "The name Alamosa means cottonwood grove." Once people came to the valley, churches weren't far behind, and Sacred Heart was one of the first in the city. The church sits just two blocks from the Rio Grande, and a visitor can sit quietly inside the cool building and enjoy a few moments' rest. "The river has always been a big part of life here in the valley," Father Jim says. "The church has too." ■

college and a career that would carry him to his current post as executive director of the state's Department of Natural Resources, Salazar lived in Manassa with 840 other people. Today there are 843. "Things change slowly in the valley," Salazar said. "I don't see it as that much different from the valley I grew up in 30 years ago."

Certainly the importance of the river hasn't changed. "The Rio Grande means everything," Salazar says. "Without the river, we don't have a San Luis Valley. It's the source of water for agriculture in the valley. Towns would dry up and die. We receive only about seven inches of rain annually in the valley. It's a desert that wasn't settled until after the Mexican-American War."

On this day in early September, Salazar is involved in a two-day conference dealing with water rights on the Rio Grande. There are county groups and regional groups here. State agencies and interstate and federal interests attend to make certain their views are heard. Agricultural and recreational needs, as well as guarantees of water for New Mexico, Texas and Mexico, play major roles in what happens. Around the edges of this and other meetings, and leading fights in the state legislature over water rights, are the lawyers. They're called "water buffaloes" in Colorado. By most accounts, they work both sides of the river, one day holding at bay challenges for the water, instituting them on another.

For water, if trite generalizations may be used, is truly the lifeblood of the valley. Taming the river in the form of diverting water for agriculture laid the foundations for a cornerstone of Colorado's economy. The Rio Grande truly is everything here. "The Indians were moved over the mountains to southwestern Colorado between 1848 and 1860," Salazar said. "Settlements began to sprout up all along the Rio Grande and its tributaries. The groups came at different times. In 1879–80, the Mormons began to come into the valley and the miners came at essentially the same time. There was a significant European influence."

Disputes over who owned the water in the Rio Grande began soon after, Salazar said, but population densities kept problems small for many years. It wasn't until much later, when downstream river users began complaining about a lack of water, that Colorado really had to deal with a restricted supply, he said. "The Rio Grande is the lifeblood for the many economies that rely on the river in Colorado, New Mexico, Texas and Mexico," Salazar said. "There's lots of competition for the water. The best way to deal with the problem is through a cooperative effort." That is bound now by the Rio Grande Compact, but things weren't always that way.

Texas and New Mexico had to file suit in the late 1960s for a settlement that required Colorado to deliver all the water set out in the compact. "Some sentiment still exists that our water is going downstream," Salazar said. "There was a lot of antagonism that water born here was going to New Mexico and Texas. There's a much better understanding today of shared water resources," Salazar said. "It's not *our* river." Of course, it would be hard to convince San Luis Valley residents—even young ones like Salazar—that the clear, snow-fed water of the Rio Grande doesn't belong more to them than anyone else. The river is, after all, fed mostly by the winter snows of the southern Rockies.

Compacts, water rights, agriculture. They are part of the lexicon of the river up here. Virtually unknown, however, is the Endangered Species Act. Salazar says that there are no endangered species relying on the Rio Grande in Colorado, but he sees the concept of *one* river as a harbinger of change for his state. It likely will defy the laws of physics and gravity and flow back up the river from New Mexico, Texas or Mexico. The day looms when just the right snail darter or riparian cactus will be listed as endangered in Texas, as some already have. That species, though, might have very specific habitat needs requiring more water be released by Colorado and New Mexico. Agriculture and recreation could suffer and hard feelings likely would rule the day.

The thought of that circumstance is plainly distasteful to Salazar, even though he shrugs and says he would do the honorable thing. "The river," he says, "flows all the way through. It's one river." ∎

JACK DEMPSEY WENT
FROM A HARDSCRABBLE
LIFE IN THE MINES OF
COLORADO TO FAME
AND FORTUNE AS A
HEAVYWEIGHT BOXER.
THE JACK DEMPSEY
MUSEUM IN MANASSA
KEEPS ALIVE THE
MEMORY OF THE
MANASSA MAULER.

# THE MANASSA MAULER

**M**ANASSA, COLO. — I honestly always thought Jack Dempsey was from New Jersey. That's where Manassa should be anyway, some hard-as-nails boxing town or maybe a Pennsylvania mill town. Not a little blinking-light, Mormon town on the flatlands of southern Colorado.

But here it is, on Highway 142, in the lower end of the San Luis Valley. I was only cutting across to get back to the Rio Grande when I was struck blind by a giant mural on the wall of an old, brick gas station. It was Dempsey, the town's big hero on the town's only gas station.

Just down the road, I came to the Jack Dempsey Museum, a one-room structure that was Dempsey's boyhood home. Inside, LaVerne King is happy to talk about the Mauler, but reluctant to submit to photographs. "I met him once, when he came back for the dedication and stayed four days," King said. "He never came back again."

Dempsey died May 31, 1983, having been proclaimed the greatest fighter of the first half of the twentieth century. He left behind surprisingly little in the way of private mementos, and the town and museum have had to make do with a few photos and things picked up here and there. "I don't know where the pictures came from," King said. "Jack said he didn't keep much of anything, the gloves from the Firpo fight and shoes from the Tunney fight." Just staying alive occupied much of people's time in Dempsey's day, and locking away some pieces of leather must have seemed a little arrogant and frivolous to him.

Manassa was home to Dempsey from his birth in June 1895 until he was 12 and his family left the valley for the mining camps on the upper Rio Grande. His parents had been among 350 Mormons who settled in Manassa around 1880, but his father left to find work in the mines. Apparently, the Mauler was born with a fighting bent and by the age of 14 was humbling miners in the camps for a dollar a fight. He performed under the

LEAVING MANASSA ON
THE WAY TO SAN LUIS,
THE DESERT FALLS
AWAY TOWARD THE
DISTANT RIO GRANDE.
OUT HERE, TRAFFIC IS
FOR THE DETERMINED,
OR THE LOST.

name "Kid Blackie." After that, fighting for real money and fame would have been easy, I suppose.

"He was well thought of," King said of Dempsey, pointing to Mauler memorabilia in the tiny museum. The entire tour takes only a couple of minutes. Photos are fine, King says, as long as she isn't in them. Reluctantly, she agrees to pose, but cuts the session short after just two shots. "That's it," King said. "If you haven't gotten it yet, you aren't getting it." ∎

# RIO GRANDE GORGE

QUESTA, N.M. — As I drive south from Alamosa and into northern New Mexico, the land begins to change. Mountains are farther apart; trees switch to pine; farmland is replaced by vast expanses of sage and juniper.

There's a seam in that sage carpet. It's the Rio Grande, cleaned up from the agricultural brown of southern Colorado to run again clean and clear. One has to trust that the river is down there at the bottom of the canyon, the edge of which can be glimpsed from time to time out near the horizon, for the rush of water and the spray of rapids can be neither seen nor heard up here on the highway. The river is always there, even though for some reason I've never been here to see it.

I always knew that Rio Grande Gorge was there, but just never knew exactly what it was: a massive rip in the flat landscape that runs for miles through northern New Mexico. It forms a gigantic canyon—now protected by the Wild and Scenic Rivers Act of 1968—that rivals anything this side of the Grand Canyon. The Rio Grande through here is clear and fast. It's fishable in spots, of course, and many people make the hike down for the day or even spend the night in one of several primitive campsites in the bottom of the canyon.

Farther down, just at the edge of the Wild Rivers Recreation Area, the Red River comes pounding in from the northeast to stoke the Rio Grande as it leaves the canyon and heads southward toward the prime kayaking and rafting territory near Taos.

I camped for the night at El Aguaje campground, right on the edge of a 570-foot dropoff into the Red River. Other camps oversee plunges of 600–700 feet into the Rio Grande itself. Well-marked trails lead down into both river canyons for hikers, and there are birds and deer for the wildlife watcher and photographer. I hiked down to the river hoping to take photos, but the canyon is so deep and the walls so steep that sunshine doesn't get down there until way up in the day. I got tired of waiting and

INSIDE RIO GRANDE
GORGE, THE RED
RIVER AND THE RIO
GRANDE COME
TOGETHER IN A BLAST
OF BLUE-GREEN
WATER.

trudged back to the top.

There are also some quite steep hills here and there on the roads inside the recreation area. That's where I encountered Tina and Evan Earl and Tina's brother Shaun Wentworth roller blading, a pursuit only for the stouthearted. They agreed to let me take pictures, while they flew down a hill with nothing between them and the pavement except some plastic rollers. Give me a car.

Wild Rivers Recreation Area is located about 25 miles north of Taos on Highway 522. It is an excellent area for hiking, camping and fishing when weather permits. No reservations are permitted, but there is an abundance of camping sites. The visitors center is open 9:00 a.m.–5:00 p.m., from Memorial Day to Labor Day. ■

## DAY FOUR

Cold front blew in big time during the night. I went out to run this morning but my hamstring hurt. Nothing is working like it should. People I wanted to visit with are unavailable. Maybe they don't know whom they're dealing with. I planned to go to the drive-in, but got tied up. Went to Alamosa wildlife refuge, but there weren't any animals or birds. Took some photos around town and then hooked it for New Mexico. Rio Grande Gorge turns out to be a wonderful place to spend the night, but it rains again and I'm stuck in the tent without company. I'm dry but the cat piss smell is driving me crazy.

FLOATING THE RIO
GRANDE BELOW
PILAR, N.M., THE
RIVER TRAVELER
GETS SPECTACULAR
VIEWS AND ENOUGH
WHITEWATER TO
SATISFY BEGINNING
THRILL SEEKERS.

# WATERBORNE AT LAST

**P**ILAR, N.M. — Crowds—by definition anything over one person I do not know—make me edgy as hell. Not the best kind of mental block for a journalist.

There have been a few times when my wife threw me out of the car so I could complete an assignment that required my wading into a throng of people. Social situations are even worse, because I can't hide behind questions and usually wind up in an argument with somebody I don't even know over something I don't even care about.

My first-ever float trip on the Rio Grande combined all the elements for one of those ugly scenes: a crowd of strangers, my tension and a youthful, outrageous statement of pseudo New Age historical adjustment. It was one of those simple, smug, unresearched beliefs that seem, if somehow given enough voice, to become fact in the urban legend category. They get passed from one head to the next until the truth of them is as solid as concrete, no longer open to question, end of discussion.

The disputed fact concerned Clayton Wetherill, who settled and explored much of southwestern Colorado and the Four Corners region of the Rocky Mountains. I was excited about having visited with his granddaughter, Carol Ann Getz, who still lived on family land along the upper Rio Grande. But when I mentioned Wetherill's name during a lull on the river, a young woman on the trip, a transplanted Californian now living in Santa Fe, let it be known that she wasn't impressed with Wetherill's exploits. The damage from his work, she said, still reverberates through the Mesa Verde country.

I know from which school she spoke those words, and even managed to hold onto my thoughts for the rest of the trip. But the ease with which she said it was stunning. There were no mitigating circumstances, no consideration for the time and the place Wetherill occupied. He found some Indian ruins and he told people about them; therefore he must have been Satan incarnate.

## DAY FIVE

*A short run today, just down to Pilar to meet the people I'll do a short float with. Still can't get anybody on the phone, but a riverside campsite is a nice place to stay. There's a pictograph on a big rock just above my tent. The campground host is from Pearsall and I hope he'll invite me for a visit, but no such luck. I bought some crackers and water from a little grocery store and inquired about a shower at the hostel in Pilar. The lady who owns it turns me down, though. Says I can stay there for $12 and get a shower, but the thing is mostly couples of women and that's a little intense and intimate for me. I have to wonder, though, because there are so many young women camping and driving in couples. Don't they have jobs? Are they involved? Lord help me.*

## DAY SIX

*Got a half-day float trip for $15 that turned out to be about two hours. Everyone else was young and seemingly amused at me. My clothes were wrong for the float. I wore my cowboy hat and my fly-fishing wading boots. Back on the road, I headed south for Taos and Santa Fe. Taos always makes me nervous. Too many people crowded around being too cool. On the way into town, I pass a car driven by a young woman with dozens of earrings and necklaces. The vehicle is the requisite Toyota station wagon with "Meat Stinks" and other vegetarian and save-the-earth stickers on it. I swear she was smoking a cigarette.*

There is little doubt that through ignorance and even meanness, European settlers of Rio Grande country drove out the American Indians, desecrated holy sites and proclaimed themselves, through manifest destiny, to be the rightful occupants of the land. Viewed through the *Dances with Wolves* glasses, there are no grays on the battlefield of history, just blacks and whites.

But Wetherill's discoveries and his work with universities and archeologists seem to be more than just looting and pillaging. He plainly knew and cared about the land and spent every free moment searching for new doors into its past. And to view him not in the context of his time in history but with an adjusted perspective based on what we know and believe nearly 100 years later is both unfair and dumb.

I'd love to know what some 20-year-old will be saying about that float trip 100 years from now. We were, after all, just one of many craft on the water that day. Some would question whether by our very presence we might not be changing forever the ecology of the river. We do after all put some of ourselves into it. We create parking lots along the Rio Grande where none existed before. Our guide, a former Texan named Matt Mitchell, spent part of his time telling about this crash or that wreck on the river, here a boater was lost, there a severed foot was found.

I doubt if even such a Hun as Clayton Wetherill ever dug out a parking lot along the edge of the river so he'd have a place to leave his van while he floated on a piece of inflated rubber and nylon. The Rio Grande runs through Santa Fe, where the same young woman worked as an architect, a delicious little irony considering each of her designs and buildings changes forever the real Rio Grande.

But I never said any of those things to her. What's the point in a senseless argument with someone I don't even know? It wouldn't change the past or the future. Or her view of it. I couldn't make Clayton Wetherill a hero or even mitigate her view of him.

I preferred instead my conversation with Mitchell, who cares about the river but in personal ways. "I really enjoy being on the river like this," Mitchell said. "There's something new every day. You have to adjust to the river and how much water is coming down. Plus, I get to be outside doing what I enjoy." Mitchell said he spent part of his childhood in Texas, before settling into the artists' community in Sante Fe. "I do mixed media work," he said, passing a postcard that features one of his drawings. "That's what I love. Rafting is what I do to survive, but it beats a real job." ■

RIVER GUIDE MATT
MITCHELL POINTS OUT
ONE OF THE MANY
PICTOGRAPHS THAT
CAN BE FOUND ALONG
THE RIO GRANDE. THIS
ONE IS JUST ABOVE
TAOS, N.M.

THIS CONVENT AND
CHURCH HAVE BEEN
A PART OF LIFE IN
ALBUQUERQUE
FROM ITS EARLIEST
SETTLEMENT DAYS.
BOTH ARE STILL
ACTIVE AND VISITORS
CAN ATTEND MASS
AT THE CHURCH.

# DON'T PRINT THAT

**A**LBUQUERQUE — I couldn't leave New Mexico without trying to deal with some of its history.

It would be a fitful cause, of course, the reduction of 400 years into one small piece of writing. But protocol demanded that something be done, and so I wandered down to Albuquerque's Old Town, the array of shops and restaurants circling the city's historical center.

The day before I had spent an uncomfortable hour driving in and around Santo Domingo Pueblo near the community of Cochiti, wanting, needing to somehow translate some of the pueblo life into written word. Photos aren't allowed at the pueblo, as signs everywhere pointed out. Just reading that sign left me feeling like an intruder. Actually having a camera and lenses in the truck seemed violative of the privacy the people who live in those American Indian communities deserve. I'd already tried to reach Bandolier National Monument from the back side, the entrance to which is near Cochiti, but had been frustrated by miles of wilderness. Now here I was driving slowly through Santo Domingo, trying not to look like a gawking gargoyle of a tourist but feeling like the embodiment of the worst meanings of the word.

I'm at once drawn to the Native American cultures sprinkled around the desert in northern New Mexico and then repelled because I suffer from discomfort at actually being around the people who live there. I fear offending them or making them feel they live in some kind of open-air zoo. I want to tell them that I am one-eighth Cherokee, as if that would make it all right to talk to them without feeling so strongly my Protestant guilt over their treatment at the hands of others of my color. But I don't. I won't.

So I slink back to I-40 and in a driving rain motor red-faced on into Albuquerque to spend the night. The next morning, a fine, sunlit, September day, finds me walking around Old Town looking for inspiration. There is a 300-year-old church and convent, but I've given myself a one-church restriction on this trip and I bagged the limit in Alamosa.

## DAY SEVEN

*Santa Fe. I camped at a KOA and it rained again during the night. Have switched from jerky to vienna sausages for most of my meals, but I did find a donut shop for a quick breakfast shot of fat and sugar. Only driving to Albuquerque today, so I veer off into the country trying to find Bandolier National Monument. It's on the Rio Grande, but I can't get there from the south side without hiking through unknown miles of wilderness area. Give up and wind up driving into an Indian pueblo where I feel very uncomfortable. Get time to run before dark and wind up eating fast-food chicken in my room again. Get sick again. They have temperature levels here that determine when people can use their fireplaces. It's because of the pollution that builds up in the valley.*

I find myself sidling up to an older lady selling silver jewelry just off the square in Old Town. I had watched her come in later than the others and set up her table around the corner from the traditional shady east side most vendors use. As I shopped for a birthday present for my wife, a crucifix, I asked why she was off the main tourist trail. "This man," said the woman, pointing to the store in whose overhang she found shelter, "lets me use this place. I don't like to be around there with those people."

She made a slight face and a dismissive wave of the hand that told more than I needed to know about how she felt toward some of the other vendors on the square. What I didn't know was why she felt that way. "They don't live in the pueblos any more," she said. "They marry people from town . . ." The sentence trailed off, but obviously some of the other sellers of jewelry had violated her sense of propriety about upholding tradition.

I ask about her jewelry. "I learned to make jewelry from my mother," the woman said. "She learned from her mother. Now I make it with my daughters and my husband. Our whole family works." No family member makes the trip down to Albuquerque each day to sell, she said, only when there's a special need or a backlog of jewelry ready for market. "I came today because my daughter is getting married. We have to feed everyone who comes [to the wedding ceremony]. I need the money."

We talk for half an hour about how the jewelry is made—it takes that long before I pump myself up enough to ask if she'd be willing to submit to a longer, more formal interview, to sit for photos for the newspaper and maybe a book. "Oh no!" she says. "I couldn't do that. My husband is on the tribal council. He wouldn't like that at all."

The conversation plainly was ended. The woman was no longer addressing me directly, but speaking to a place in the distance, past my left shoulder. She didn't tell me to leave. That would have been a breach of her own etiquette. It was up to me to deal with my end of it. She'd already moved to another place, leaving only her earthly body for me to speak to.

She did have a crucifix for sale, and I made a feeble excuse about having some other errands to run but planning to stop back by on my way out of the plaza and pick it up. We both knew that was a lie, I think. I couldn't face her again. I think it was embarrassment over the eagerness I had shown at thinking I could penetrate for a moment her space and learn something of her and her life. I slipped away to the church. But it was an empty experience, a meaningless side trip on the route back to my truck. I had to get away. And I did. ■

BY THE TIME THE
RIO GRANDE MAKES
ITS WAY INTO
ALBUQUERQUE, N.M.,
IT HAS SPREAD OUT
INTO THE SHALLOW,
SANDY STREAM
MOST PEOPLE KNOW.
THIS VIEW OF
THE RIVER IS FROM
THE RIO GRANDE
NATURE CENTER IN
ALBUQUERQUE.

GARY STOLZ STANDS
AT THE EDGE OF
THE RIO GRANDE AT
BOSQUE DEL APACHE.
UNFORTUNATELY,
THE RIVER HAS BEEN
SO CHANGED BY
CHANNELIZATION THAT
ALL THE WORK AT
BOSQUE DEL APACHE
HAS BEEN TO TRY TO
RESTORE AND RE-CREATE
AN AREA THAT HUMANS
WIPED OUT.

# BOSQUE DEL APACHE

SOCORRO, N.M. — The Rio Grande leaves Albuquerque looking very much like the river of legend. Broad, shallow and silty, it meanders out through the New Mexican desert, seemingly with no clear purpose other than to meet the demands of gravity and physics by flowing south, maybe just to get things over with.

Irrigation channels carry most of the actual water, a shock to the uninformed because there's little that grows out here except scrub brush. The channels run alongside the actual Rio Grande, dug narrow and deep to prevent seepage and evaporation loss.

A few cottonwoods and some minor agriculture mark the river's path paralleling Interstate 25, but there's not much else. Even the surprise down the road from Albuquerque doesn't look like much until you get inside it. Bosque del Apache National Wildlife Refuge is a monument to nature's ability to utilize tools at hand and, with a little help, establish a natural way station where none existed.

Bosque del Apache explodes each fall and spring in a spray of feathers. Sandhill cranes are the major winter inhabitants, and they are celebrated each November with the Festival of the Cranes. People stream in to watch the arrival of the majority of the 17,000-plus sandhills that winter on the refuge and surrounding country. But there are also a few transplanted whooping cranes, eagles and hawks, pelicans, ducks, geese and migrating songbirds—325 species of birds altogether. Another 75 species of mammals, including mule deer, coyotes and wild turkeys, hang around all the time.

The amazing thing about the desert here is that it celebrates the marvels of water and the explosion of life in one of the federal refuge systems' biggest success stories. "This was not a traditional wetland," said Gary Stolz, a biologist working at Bosque del Apache who took time to drive me around the area and offered me a room for the night. "It is the flood plain of the Rio Grande,

## DAYS EIGHT & NINE

*Drive only short distance again, this time down to Bosque del Apache National Wildlife Refuge. Coyotes were everywhere in the refuge. They plainly are making a pretty good living off the birds that live in there. Mosquitoes were incredible. Big and aggressive. Ran at dusk and had the place all to myself. Back up the road a few miles in San Antonio, the Owl Cafe serves up famous green chili cheeseburgers and french fries. Cold Coors Light tastes real good. Leaving Bosque del Apache and dropping down off the plateau and heading toward El Paso. The river swings in close and then slides away from the road here. Far to the south, I can see the jagged edges of the tail end of the Rockies. Country no longer looks like high desert, just desert. RV caravans in full swing. Had to coast down hills to save gas but made it to El Paso before dark. Feels good to be back in Texas.*

which was historically intermittent. There was just the river and the strip of trees along it." Those strips of trees, cottonwoods mostly, are known as bosques, hence the name.

Back up the highway in Albuquerque is the Rio Grande Nature Center, a 270-acre state park anchored by a cottonwood grove, the last native cottonwood bosque left in the western United States, according to park manager Karen Brown. Channelization, Cochiti Lake Dam and agriculture doomed most of the cottonwoods in central New Mexico, Brown said, as well as much of the Rio Grande itself. "The river channel here looks more like the real river," she said, "but it still doesn't flood enough. What we have here is as close as we can get to the real thing at this point. We have a lot of invasive species that we're trying to keep out, but that's hard too."

Those invasive species—Russian olive, salt cedar (tamarisk) and Chinese elm—are common and hated along the Rio Grande. "The river through the city has always been kind of a dumping ground," Brown said. "People also gathered wood down there and used it for target practice. As the city grew, problems with the river grew."

Management of the river isn't necessarily management for the river. Taming it robbed the Rio Grande of its identity and the nearby plants and animals of its periodic flooding forays into the countryside. Everything suffered. "We're never going to have a river like it used to be," Brown said. "It's never going to be a natural river and flow the way it did a hundred years ago. The river is completely channelized. We're trying to do the best we can with what's left."

At Bosque del Apache as well, it was the canal system, built to aid agricultural irrigation, that created some of the problems the river suffers here and that is now being used to turn the plain into a wildlife haven. "When the river was put into canals, it changed the landscape," Stolz said. Naturally slow and shallow with occasional floods, the Rio Grande became not much more than a wide breach in the desert. Invasive exotic plant species, Russian olive and the dreaded salt cedar, spread along the edges and eventually into the riverbed itself, choking out and replacing the wildlife-friendly, but flood-dependent, cottonwoods.

One need only to fly along the river's course to be able to see that salt cedar isn't only a refuge problem. It has taken over in dense monocultures in many areas, but trees within the refuge are 30 feet high and so thick that only bulldozers can break them

A MULE DEER
FEEDS AT THE
EDGE OF ONE OF
THE PONDS INSIDE
THE BOSQUE DEL
APACHE REFUGE.

**SNOW
GEESE
WINTER AT
BOSQUE
DEL
APACHE,
TOO.**

up. And the damage doesn't stop with the tree itself. Salt cedar is water dependent, though it can't live in water. Efficient root systems siphon off water before other plants can get to it. Then the cedar replaces the water with salt, thus rendering the land useless for anything other than salt cedar.

The cycle is vicious and deadly in terms of the natural flora along the river. "The cottonwoods haven't been able to grow since the salt cedar got started, and all we have are old, decadent trees that don't offer the same benefits younger, dynamic trees would," Stolz told me. Habitat-specific species—willow flycatchers and the meadow jumping mouse—that depended on the riverside growth of cottonwoods and associated plants are struggling to hang on. In the river itself, the shovelnose sturgeon, longnose gar, speckled chub, blue sucker and Rio Grande shiner have ceased to exist.

So within the refuge, workers are clearing great patches of salt cedar and replanting with young cottonwoods. The refuge canal system now is used to move water around inside the 7,000-acre area that comprises the riparian portion of the 57,000-acre refuge.

Bosque del Apache was born as a refuge in 1938 with just 17 sandhill cranes to mark its arrival. Amazingly enough, there had been no natural wetland in this location; there was just a rare vision that something could be created from nothing, using mostly the waters of the Rio Grande. And the concept has worked, practically and otherwise. I've heard rumblings of similar trials along the Rio Grande in Texas and Mexico, of hopes that long, hostile and isolated stretches of the river will be claimed by humans in the name of wildlife. Sounds like a plan. ∎

# SONGDOG SERENADE

This is a story—almost a sermon—about coyotes, which I like, and people, about whom I have mixed feelings. It starts and ends with a pile of snow goose feathers at Bosque del Apache National Wildlife Refuge.

The Rio Grande, especially once it reaches into more arid country, is a natural home for coyotes. They come not for its water, though they will drink it, nor for its shade, though they might linger there on a hot noonday. Coyotes come to the Rio Grande for the animals: mice and rats, armadillos, rabbits, lizards and snakes, deer, turkeys and other birds, sheep, goats, dogs and cats. The coyote is an equal opportunity predator.

There's no malice in his hunting, of course, and no regrets, if an animal could feel such. There's just the drive to survive, propagate the species and die, adding back to the system some protein, minerals and calcium. He's damn good at it, too, having survived the worst forms of human persecution in the name of animal husbandry to survive and thrive. I have lain in sleeping bags and fancy beds, listening to the yipping and howling that have earned for the determined canine the nickname "Songdog." It's a delicious irony that coyotes now live quite comfortably in and around some of the largest cities west of the Mississippi.

It's his hunting that links me to the coyote. I hunt. I have shot coyotes in my day, in the name of saving a few white-tailed deer, which I also hunt. But I have come to peace with and embraced that part of me that hunts. It throbs inside of me as strongly and inevitably as in any coyote. It was with me when I was born in Marshall, Texas, after World War II, passed along by my father and grandfather from their Indian ancestors who got it from some guy in a cave.

I will carry it with me when I die and my ashes are scattered (I have asked that I be loaded into a shotgun shell and flung at a quail or a dove) on the south Texas desert to put back my own feeble offering of protein and calcium and minerals. I could stand to have my carcass thrown out near a coyote den, but my family is struggling with the ashes in the shotgun shell concept so I won't push it.

The problem here is that the coyote and I are hunters in a world increasingly unaccepting of hunting. He'll survive better than I, because no law, no trespass barrier, no amount of human scorn will stop him from hunting. That's his job.

Human hunters, on the other hand, have to contend with the notion that they can and should be that which they are not. From Disney movies to seances and feel-good seminars, the late twentieth century is rolling on a sea of delusion that the world is just a happy place gone wrong. If we wish enough, the theory goes, we can live in a world where lions lie down with lambs and grizzly bears don't eat fish. And coyotes don't eat snow geese.

My wife, Rana, and I were visiting Bosque del Apache at the height of the snow goose migration. We were not the only humans there, which gave me the chance to indulge myself to a series of typically superior views of people who want to watch the birdies but who have no concept of what's really going on out there.

We photographed a bald eagle zooming in low over the geese and no one else there seemed to understand he was forcing them to fly so that he could watch for the stragglers and cripples that would make up his next meal. When he landed in shallow water, other people talked and laughed so loud that the eagle left. They didn't understand why.

And finally, I overheard a remark about the piles of feathers that were everywhere on the levees in the refuge. The visitor wondered what caused them to be there. There were no bones, just the feathers. That's a sign of a coyote. He eats the whole thing. A bobcat would leave certain things behind, bones and gizzards. An eagle or an owl would fly away with the bird to some other dining location. The coyote, though, eats on the run. He might charge into the geese at night, when the white feathers and constant raucous jockeying for position on the roost would make them easy to find and chase. Any slow-moving bird will be snapped up and carried to the levee for a quick meal. If there are young ones at home, the food will be converted to milk or regurgitated in pieces. Then the coyote hunts again.

Coyotes and people are not that different. We do what we do—hunt, eat, fight, love and die—and it's all part of the plan.

The difference is that the coyote isn't trying to change the plan. ■

**A BALD
EAGLE
SWOOPS
ACROSS A
SMALL LAKE
AT BOSQUE
DEL APACHE.**

# LAST OF THE CRANES

SOCORRO, N.M. — Whooping cranes evoke deep, incredibly strong emotions in people.

The overwhelming feeling I had on seeing one at Bosque del Apache National Wildlife Refuge, the thought that ran through my head, was this: "They aren't going to make it." No amount of money, no New Age crystal gazing, no raft of prayers sent skyward on black-tipped wings can stop this boulder from crashing at the bottom of the cliff.

My epiphanous crane was a single, white whooper awash in a sea of gray sandhill cranes. He (I use that pronoun to avoid the distasteful "it") is one of the leftovers in a failed experiment involving stolen eggs, sandhill foster parents and a desperate U.S. Fish and Wildlife Service willing to do almost anything to save the symbol of endangered species work in North America.

Their plan was a simple one, really. Whoopers generally lay two eggs but hatch and raise only one. The second egg is a backup. Biologists hoped that they could steal one egg from each successful nest and slide it into a nest tended by a sandhill crane. The sandhills, which numbers many thousands, would in avian parenting theory raise the whooper as their own. The whoopers, meanwhile, still would care for their remaining egg and if everything worked according to plan the number of wild whooping cranes could be increased.

Well, the sandhills honestly raised the young whoopers, and the single crane I saw was one of six that wintered on the refuge during the winter of 1993–94. The problem with the plan, though, was that the whooping cranes couldn't read the wildlife service's prospectus. They survived but think they are sandhill cranes. Maybe that doesn't prove that environment is everything, but it certainly makes a case for it. Without other whooping cranes to teach them proper mating behavior for their kind, the young whoopers fell in with their sandhill cousins, producing something that the service jokingly calls "whoophills."

Whooping cranes, meanwhile, continue a precarious existence on the edge of extinction. Their numbers have climbed to around 150, but that seems to be the ceiling. Best counts showed that 143 of the birds wintered on the Texas Gulf Coast in 1993–94, but when the flock headed north for their wintering grounds near the Arctic Circle, only 135–138 were expected to make the trip. One or two get lost every year on the trip and each summer's hatch just barely keeps the flock at level numbers.

The Texas flock knows nothing of the scattering of whoopers flying with the sandhills in New Mexico. Both are attuned to their own internal calendar and compass, and that's really what struck me so about the whooping crane I saw. It was like a fist to the stomach.

My wife and I were making a mad dash down the Rio Grande to take new photos and let her see some of what I'd seen when I made the same trip alone. The tote board in the refuge headquarters noted that six whoopers were on the refuge, along with sandhills, most brands of ducks, bald eagles and other raptors. We drove around the refuge, stopping for photos and marveling at the sights and sounds.

Late on the first afternoon, we stopped near one pond and stood outside the car to soak up the unbelievable sounds of the sandhills coming back to the refuge to roost for the night. Light had already dropped below the point of photographs when we noticed a lone, white bird well off to the side of the main flock of gray sandhills feeding in the shallow water. Binoculars proved what we already suspected: a whooping crane, the second I'd ever seen. The first had been a tangle of broken bones and bloody feathers, shot by a drunken heathen trying to win an ill-fated bet over his shooting ability.

This bird was alive, of course, but my feelings weren't much different about him. He seemed, in my anthropomorphic state, so lonely, so unaware of his plight, so doomed. Of course, he wasn't alone. He was with 16,000 sandhill cranes he thought were his ordained running mates. The loneliness was all mine and it was awful.

Driving south from Socorro the next day, I offered to my wife my theory that whooping cranes weren't going to make it. All the millions of dollars and the countless manhours—volunteer and otherwise—won't be enough to save them, I said. She viewed that as a potentially dangerous thing to say about the international symbol of species restoration. Just the kind of thing lots of people think, but only crazy people like me will actually say out loud.

I have a friend, Ray Sasser, who, in a fit of black humor, once said the Fish and Wildlife Service ought to admit whooping cranes are doomed. Then they could auction off the rights to hunt the remaining 150 or so for really big money to people in the habit of collecting rare and beautiful things. The money raised could then be put into saving some animal that really has a chance to survive.

That won't ever happen, but some realistic talk about whooping cranes might be more beneficial than pretending that we're saving them. They were abused at a time when the words *endangered species* meant nothing to anybody. Maybe in the grand scheme of things, whooping cranes didn't have what it takes to survive. Sandhills have prospered, after all; whoopers have not.

What do I believe about whooping cranes and the future? I'm not sure. They are beautiful, delicate and wonderful birds and I hope they make it. I don't think they will. Certainly not that we should give up. Maybe we should go to captive breeding, take the birds out of the wild and at least save something. Maybe all the twenty-first-century whoopers will live in zoos. Maybe we need to develop a new species, whoopers crossed with sandhills, that keeps some of the bloodlines alive. Maybe one tiny parasite comes along and stamps out the entire wild flock and we never know why.

If a whooping crane falls in a Texas marsh, does it make a sound? ■

# RHYMES WITH WITCH

WHEN THE RIO
GRANDE LEAVES
ELEPHANT BUTTE,
IT ONCE AGAIN
IS A CLEAR,
FAST-MOVING
STREAM. THAT
DOESN'T LAST
LONG, THOUGH.
THE DESERT
ABOVE EL PASO
AND TREMENDOUS
HUMAN DEMANDS
ON RIVER WATER
QUICKLY CHANGE
IT BACK TO
A SHALLOW,
DIRTY RIVER.

EL PASO — The Rio Grande in this border city stinks. It's dirty and polluted, decorated with rusty car bodies and floating plastic oil jugs.

And now for the bad news: the Rio Grande—from El Paso to below Fort Hancock, a distance of more than 60 miles—isn't even a river. It's a glorified drainage ditch, featuring a channelized, concrete border drainage and a system of canals and dams. The Rio Grande doesn't become a river again for an embarrassing 200 miles when the Rio Conchos flows in from Mexico.

Perhaps the hardest part of this ugly scene to deal with is the sense of resignation about it, even from people who seem to be caring and understanding of its former beauty and constant importance to the peoples of two countries. "It will never be a natural river again," I was told by Robin Smith, an environmental expert with the International Boundary and Water Commission in El Paso. "It's a channelized river. There is no terrestrial or aquatic habitat threatened in this part of the river because there is none."

With that view as the standard, nothing is being done with the river except to make the canals and channels more efficient. Basically, the whole thing is operating under a 50-year-old management plan aimed at pulling water out of the river for human use. It continues because it is there and because staggering growth in the valley, in the cities of Juarez and El Paso, are putting incredible demands on the river. It serves as sewer and water supply at the same time.

But even that isn't necessarily the problem. Jugs and dirt and sewage can be cleaned up, Smith said, but the channelization, begun nearly 100 years ago, is a done deal. The river of legend, the big river, is just one big mess. Alteration of the river throughout its run from Colorado to the Gulf of Mexico is a part of history, of course. European settlers took that "change it, tame it" mentality wherever they went. It was what they did and I have a

A RAINBOW SPANS
THE RIO GRANDE AT
EL PASO, ONE OF
THOSE FEEL-GOOD
SIGNS FROM HEAVEN
THAT STRIKE
WANNABE DO-GOODERS
BUT DON'T MEAN
ANYTHING TO THE
PEOPLE TRYING TO
SCRATCH OUT A
LIVING FROM THE
MEAGER LAND ALONG
THE RIVER.

hard time criticizing them for it. But the damage that lingers in its wake is hard to take.

Huge impoundments such as Elephant Butte and Caballo, north of El Paso in New Mexico, tamed the periodic flooding that washed away crops and homes in El Paso, but the change in flow allowed noxious plants to gain a foothold in the fragile river environment. Dissolved salts in the riverbed itself have increased over the years, leaving the water quality worse than ever. But the channelization made the greatest impact, putting most of the water into ditches in El Paso. The river bed was narrowed and deepened to facilitate the flow and stop evaporation loss. Then a flood-control levee was built on both sides of the river to stop any flooding that might occur. Where the river once meandered around as wild rivers do, changing the international border from time to time, the Rio Grande now runs in a very straight channel. Twenty miles below El Paso, the river disappears into a water treatment plant.

Not far from there, I found Angie's Cafe, the kind of place county commissioners go for coffee, tea and Mexican food, the west Texas power lunch. A steady stream of Hudspeth County's 2,900 residents move through the little dining room that sits just below Interstate 10, maybe two miles above the Rio Grande. Among the visitors are sheriff's deputies and Border Patrol officers, truck drivers and ranchers. Table talk is of who's sick of traveling and whether the going rate for illegal alien work in the old days was 60 cents or 80 cents an hour. At a nearby table, two guys share pecan pie and debate how long it will take them to reach New Orleans. An elderly couple from California want to know if they can get some of that hot sauce they've heard so much about.

Through it all, Angie wanders in and out from the kitchen to visit, while her daughter Bridgett waits tables. Hudspeth County commissioner Lester Ray Talley, with whom I have come to visit, is running late, so Bridgett brings out a basket of chips and some salsa, "so you'll have something to do. Want me to call him for you?" Just as she picks up the phone, though, Talley walks in the door, all plaid shirt and straw hat, greeting everyone in the cafe. Coffee appears and the talk begins.

"Well, it was a mighty big river when I was growing up, but it's not so big now," said Talley, 64. "My dad came out [in 1934] and found work, and a year later we moved out from Corsicana. Those were hard times back then and he was looking for work."

## DAY TEN

*Old friends Terry and Frank Bertling take me in for a couple of nights in El Paso. I hired Terry for her first newspaper job, but she's done the rest for herself. It's nice to share a beer and a taco with friends; Frank and Terry are great to be with. They take me to the nether world of El Paso, where the international border is just a stake in the ground and people cross at will. The river, by the way, is just a muddy and ugly piece of junk here. When the wind is right, you can smell the raw sewage from Juarez. Visit area across the river, but still in Texas that is used as staging area for illegal crossing and drug deals. People are coming and going like jaywalkers.*

The elder Talley found work for wages and then as a sharecropper on a farm. After saving his money, he was able to buy his own land and farm. The depression was the depression, even on a farm in far west Texas. "It was just hard. We worked for 75 cents to a dollar a day on the farms."

But the Rio Grande in those days was still a river. "Back then, the river was crooked," Talley said. "They straightened it out and changed it." One change was a flood out of Elephant Butte in 1942 that Talley believes brought the first salt cedar to the area below El Paso. "We didn't have any before that, but then we got the drought that started in 1950 and it just kept closing in. Now the river is not even eight or 10 feet wide in some places. It's not good for anything. It used to be a good place to fish. Now raw sewage comes in from Mexico and it's kind of dangerous to eat a fish down there. We've lost stock on it in June when the water gets real low. They go down to drink, go lie down and never get up. It bothers me what has happened to the river."

As it should. Being on and around the river at El Paso is just a bad feeling. It's a hospital visit to a patient everyone is saying won't survive. This is the way it is, they say, and nothing's going to change it. There are just too many people and too many demands. But the original proposal for a canal expansion underway in 1993 dated back 60 years. The IBWC doesn't see that as managing backwards, "just for a different use," as one official told me. Every drop of water coming into El Paso is allocated to someone or something, and canals and channels help hold onto it so everyone can get at it, like jackals fighting over a carcass.

People throw around numbers: 2 million people in El Paso/Juarez today, 5 million in the next 50 years; 43 percent of water leaving Elephant Butte allocated for Texas use; 50-year-old management plans; two counties. They forget the most important number, though, *one*, as in one river. The Rio Grande—right here it just plain sucks. ■

ELEPHANT BUTTE
RESERVOIR NEAR
TRUTH OR
CONSEQUENCES,
N.M., WAS ONE OF
THE FIRST GIANT
LAKES BUILT ON THE
RIO GRANDE AND
ONE THAT CHANGED
THE RIVER FOREVER.

THE BORDER PATROL
HAS GIVEN UP TRYING
TO CATCH ILLEGAL
ALIENS ONCE THEY'VE
CROSSED THE RIVER.
A COMPLETE BLOCKADE
OF THE RIVER HAS
WORKED FOR U.S.
CITIZENS, BUT HAS
ANGERED RESIDENTS
OF JUAREZ ON THE
OPPOSITE SIDE.

# DOWN ON THE BORDER

EL PASO — The Rio Grande as international border somehow seems an arbitrarily lousy line of demarcation.

Even the series of white pillars that mark the rest of the border between the United States and Mexico doesn't strike me as wrong the way using the Rio Grande does. Historically, Mexicans and Americans both had a loose and easy approach to the river border, especially in its early stages around El Paso. Part of the El Paso tourist trail was a trip down to the Rio Grande to watch the parade of runners, walkers, waders and floaters try to beat the odds—and the U.S. Border Patrol—in a dash from Mexico into Texas.

I've watched the crossings from El Paso restaurant patios. Two or three, maybe half a dozen Mexicans sneak out of a culvert or clump of brush, staying together for safety and support but ready to scatter at the sight of Border Patrol agents. Confusion can be a friend.

Some made it, some didn't. That was part of the game: Try to slip across and disappear in the city or ride the Border Patrol bus back to Juarez and try again another day. But as things in Mexico got tougher and the land of dreams north of the river seemed even more golden, the game ceased to be a game. The rush of illegal aliens crossing into Texas became a flood. "We were recording 800 to 1,000 apprehensions daily in the 20-mile area of river in the El Paso district," said Doug Mosier, public information officer for the Border Patrol. "Something had to be done."

Enter the human blockade, a round-the-clock, seven-day stratagem that will become the Border Patrol's new way of cutting down on the number of illegal crossings. In the 20-mile stretch at El Paso, agents in cars are stationed at every known crossing and bridge area, usually 200 to 500 yards apart on the Texas side of the river. Despite angry protests in Juarez, the program has worked, if success can be measured in the number of Mexicans not crossing the border. In the first 18 days of the program, the district recorded 2,883 apprehensions. In the same time period in 1992, the Border Patrol made 14,800 apprehensions.

One can only guess at the real number of undocumented aliens who found their way safely into Texas and other states. Through most of this century, they were an accepted part of life and virtually no south or west Texas ranch was without at least one undocumented alien. Somewhere along the way, their crossing became a part of the language. *Wetback*, sometimes shortened to *wet*, was first a literal description of the river crossers, often an epithet, and now politically incorrect slang.

There seemed no real reason to stop the movement completely. It was accepted that ranchers and farmers need the cheap labor to survive. So, in a city like El Paso, where history is rooted as much in Mexico as in Texas, and where many citizens have family just across the international bridge, the Rio Grande became a boundary recognized mostly on maps. That's easy to understand, too, since residents of Juarez in Mexico could see prosperity, hope and

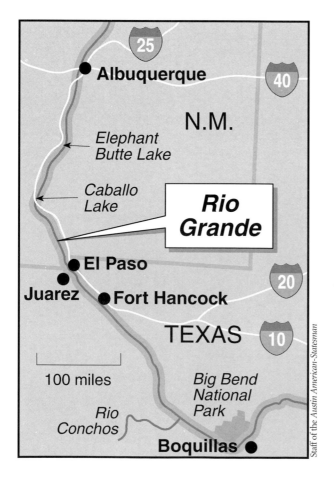

A MULE DEER
DOE KEEPS
WATCH AS
HER FAWN
BREAKS FOR
COVER IN A
BUSHY
CANYON IN
BIG BEND
NATIONAL
PARK.

BEING ALONE IN THE
DESERT CAN HAVE
STRANGE EFFECTS ON
SOME PEOPLE. I FOUND
THIS CLOUD—FLOATING
OVER MEXICO—A
WONDERFUL THING,
EVEN THOUGH I WAS
LOST AND LONELY.

city services just a few yards away to the north. Coming north to find work, save money and improve one's lot became an accepted way of life.

By 1992, however, the numbers had swelled to the breaking point for the Border Patrol and the citizens of El Paso, Mosier said. "It fluctuated from year to year for a long time, but the last two years the numbers just exploded. In fiscal year 1993, there were 285,000 illegal aliens caught in this district."

The new program was born of that staggering work load, Mosier said. "It concentrates our manpower and puts people at strategic places where we normally see illegal aliens coming into the U.S.," he said. "The idea is to stop them from coming in, as opposed to trying to catch them once they're on U.S. soil."

Agents were moved from the interior and restationed at the border, Mosier said. There they use the standard tools of the trade—night scopes, sensors, helicopters and foot speed. "It essentially walls off the river and it has worked fantastically," he said. "We're going to maintain it indefinitely."

Of course, human beings adapt and Mexican residents trying to cross illegally are doing just that, Mosier said. "The old thing was you'd see 50 or 60 people staged up over there to charge across and try to make it. You'd see people who would ferry people across for a fee," he said. "Now we're starting to see some night crossings, which we rarely saw in the old days."

One El Paso resident, while acknowledging that the blockade was working, expressed some disappointment at the change. "It was kind of neat to see them come across," she said. "They'd use big inner tubes to float across sometimes and come right up and cut the fence and head across the highway."

Mosier, however, isn't missing the old days at all. "This strategy has worked very well," he said. "In a way, the river begs to be crossed, but this is the best way to stop it."

My friends Terry and Frank Bertling, who live in El Paso, drove me down back roads on the city's west side to a parking area near one of the international boundary markers. We watched as Juarez residents rode bicycles through the brush to the pavement and I assume to some destination in El Paso. They would pause long enough to assess our vehicle as having nothing to do with the Border Patrol and then move on, invisible even before they were out of sight. ■

## DAY ELEVEN

*El Paso is a fascinating city. Dinner on a patio at a riverside cafe is preceded by a few minutes of watching people cross the river at dusk. From talking with people who live here, it's pretty plain they don't consider themselves really a part of Texas. Saw the biggest white-winged doves I've ever seen and later find out they are a kind of mini-subspecies that lives no place else. Frank and Terry have a rock yard. No mowing. My kind of place.*

ANOTHER EXAMPLE OF
FISCAL RESPONSIBILITY
BY OUR FRIENDS
IN THE FEDERAL
GOVERNMENT. BLIMPS
LIKE THIS ONE ARE
SUPPOSED TO KEEP
UP WITH ILLEGAL DRUG
TRAFFIC ACROSS THE
RIO GRANDE, BUT THEY
STAY BROKEN DOWN
AND INOPERABLE
MOST OF THE TIME.
BUT THINK OF ALL THE
JOBS THEY PROVIDE.

# FLOAT LIKE A DRUG BLIMP, STING LIKE A BEE

**M**ARATHON — There may never have been an international border so loosely viewed and often crossed as the river corridor between Texas and Mexico. People, drugs, money, all flow back and forth with an easy liquidity, even if most of the drugs run north and the money runs south.

The drugs and people were commodities Mexico had in abundance to meet the requirements of a supply-and-demand economy in the United States. And that's okay, because the success in importing both represents the governmental futility in trying to legislate against either human beings' ingenuity or personal desires. If there's a demand, there will be a supply, and if there's a delivery problem, it will be overcome.

I was struck by the similarity between two ridiculous attempts by government to deal with border migration northward, namely those involving Africanized bees and drugs. Drugs, of course, have been streaming into Texas from Mexico for who knows how long. The bees, "killer bees," were newly arrived in 1991. I know more scientific data about the bees, but I have stronger feelings about the drugs.

Spend any time on the Texas border these days and you'll eventually see one of the federal government's "drug blimps," small versions of passenger craft that are supposed to rise up over the desert on tethers to keep track of illegal drug traffic across the Rio Grande. Somewhere, someplace, some faceless bureaucrat is laughing his butt off at this financial disaster. Even if it worked, it wouldn't work, but the blimps are forever on the ground, inflated, sitting and waiting to be floated up to track bad guys. As soon as they go up, though, the tethers break, the blimps crash, and DEA officers come running out to make sure the sensitive equipment isn't stolen or lost.

The drug blimp boondoggle is the biggest joke going in the deer and cattle camps of south and west Texas. I refuse to ask how much the program costs or how many drug planes have

## DAYS TWELVE & THIRTEEN

*Rana drove west from Burnet and I drove east from El Paso. We met in Odessa for two days and had a nice weekend. Downtown Midland looks like a ghost town, but the loop area is booming. I leave Rana and head down through Marathon to Big Bend National Park. Sage is blooming and the desert is beautiful, but hard on my allergies.*

been caught. I prefer the humorous view of it, rather than having to deal with the reality of people pretending they are doing something other than spending money on toys that could be used to help restore the Rio Grande to some of its former glory. They'd save even more money if they simply legalized and controlled the stuff, but that would be too simple.

Drugs are an issue, a campaign issue, and as such they won't be forgotten as a way to make statements to voters willing to believe that the right politician and the right amount of money will work some miracle on the human compulsion to escape or feel good. Throw money at it and the problem will go away, floating like a loose blimp on a Mexican west wind. I don't think much of the law-and-order approach to drugs, which puts me in a strange place in contrast with many of the folks with whom I hunt and fish: I favor legalizing drugs and controlling handguns. I'm not sure what to think about killer bees, except that no government plan can stop them, either. They are streaming across the border and spreading out into Texas.

Thanks in large part to a protracted, doomsday media tracking of their northward migration, not to mention movie depictions of major cities knocked to their knees by rampaging "killer" bees, we citizens of Texas could be forgiven our dismay when Africanized honeybees crossed the border in the fall of 1991. But are the hybridized and aggressive insects as dangerous as their Hollywood big-screen counterparts? "Is a bluebird blue?" said Wayland Chandler, an inspector for Texas A&M University's extension service. "I've killed thousands of those colonies and they are dangerous. I've seen horses that they killed."

On the other hand, maybe they aren't so dangerous. The bees have caused their share of problems and consternation in the years since they arrived in Texas, but they haven't really left a trail of carnage in their wake, according to Kathleen Davis, a spokesperson with the agriculture department at Texas A&M. "We have had one confirmed fatality from Africanized bee stings in Texas," Davis said, "an 82-year-old man in Rio Grande City last year." She pointed out that there were two deaths in 1993 as a result of stings from European honeybees, the more passive honeybee most Texans come into contact with.

Texas A&M is tracking the progress of the bees as they expand their territory, Davis said, and has made continuing education efforts aimed at protecting the public. Trouble-shooters like Chandler wipe out the bees when they can be located, but beyond that, the current Texas and U.S. bee policy is one of wait and see. "They actually arrived in Texas in October of 1990," Davis said. The insects, Africanized honeybees that had migrated from Brazil, were originally being studied in hopes that the more aggressive, faster-breeding strain could be used to increase honey production.

But their extremely aggressive nature, which manifests itself in attacks by massive numbers of bees willing to chase a subject for long distances, proved too much for beekeepers to deal with. When the bees escaped in 1957, they began a migration that carried them up through Central America and Mexico and to the United States. Africanized bees are now found well up into Texas, New Mexico and Arizona and within one mile of California, Davis said. "There are theories that they could go all the way to Canada in warm winters and that they are as far north as they can stand," she said.

In Texas, the bees have made their way into the Big Bend region of Texas and as far north as San Angelo; they have been confirmed in Travis County and even 35 miles west of Houston. Most recent checks have shown a slight slowdown in their spread, Davis said, but there isn't enough information available to know if that means anything. To keep tabs on their movements, A&M scientists have placed special boxes along highways throughout the state. Those are the blue plastic boxes you see hanging from trees. They contain a special pheromone that attracts bee colonies that then are trapped in the boxes. Pheromones are chemical substances produced by animals that trigger such responses as mating and feeding. They are also responsible for the killer bees' legendary aggression and tenacity. When one bee stings, he releases a pheromone that signals the attack to other bees.

"As long as they can smell that pheromone, they'll keep chasing the object," Davis said. "They smell it and target that area." That explains why one person or animal may be stung hundreds of times, while others in the area escape virtually unharmed. The bees release the stinger when they attack, Davis said. "It's actually the entire back end of their bodies. Then they go off and bleed to death. The sting is fatal to them." The sting itself isn't any more dangerous than that of other bees, she said, unless the individual is allergic to insect stings.

"The problem is they attack in greater numbers," Davis said. "They will pursue someone for half a mile." The pursuit makes

OUR RIO GRANDE
CAMP ON THE MEXICO
SIDE OF THE RIVER.
WE SPENT THE NIGHT
LISTENING TO THE
CLICKS AND CLACKS
OF BATS SUCKING UP
MOSQUITOES IN THE
CANYON ABOVE
THE RIVER.

the elderly and young more susceptible to severe stings, she said, since they have a harder time escaping the swarm. "They are very sensitive to noise," Chandler said, and that's normally what triggers the attack. Barking dogs, lawn mowers, bulldozers, hammering or sawing can bring on the bees. "And they don't give you any warning," he said. "They just come on you."

Africanized bees multiply quickly and thus produce more queens and swarms than European bees, Davis said. "They just keep flying until they find an area that has the elements they need: water, blooming plants, etc." When the swarm reaches an area not already populated by other bees, they'll set up a nest in quiet, out-of-the-way places. "They like old, abandoned buildings, pipes, tires, 55-gallon drums, things like that," Davis said. "We had one man in Brownsville stung several hundred times by a colony that had moved into his deer blind." Nests are much larger than those of regular honeybees, which accounts for the greater productivity in terms of honey. "The average size is about 60,000 bees, but some are six feet long and have several hundred thousand bees," she said. "The bees themselves are actually slightly smaller, but you can't tell with the naked eye."

Davis said the bees don't target humans for their attacks, but still have stung 191 people in Texas with one fatality. There have been at least 31 animals attacked, with 19 of those killed.

Now here's where it all gets weird. We spend all this money fighting something that people want and are getting anyway, namely the drugs, without being able to do anything more than help its transporters create more ingenious ways of delivering it. With the bees, we just watch and wait and hope to control the situation as it goes along. It doesn't make sense. I know philosophers and zealots will be able to shoot holes in the logic I've applied and God only knows there's a stretch between bees and drugs, but, hey, my plan couldn't do worse. ■

JIM CARRICO STRAINS
AGAINST THE OARS OF
HIS RAFT DURING A
FLOAT TRIP THROUGH
THE BIG BEND
COUNTRY OF WEST
TEXAS. THE RIVER
HERE IS POLLUTED
AND SHALLOW, BUT
STILL WILD AND IN
KEEPING WITH THE
RUGGED LAND
AROUND IT.

# THE RIVER AT LAST

**R**IO GRANDE VILLAGE — I was only marginally looking forward to spending three days floating on the Rio Grande.

My previous float experience hadn't been all that positive. An unhappy overnighter on the Salmon River with my wife and sister-in-law many years ago had just about turned me against any river outing not centered around fishing. And then a "half-day" trip farther back up the Rio Grande had cost me $45 for a couple of hours and had given me little sense of the river itself.

But after a couple of weeks of sleeping alone on the ground, nobody to talk to but myself, I needed some company and I needed the story of the Rio Grande in the Big Bend country. After the ugly insensibilities of what's being done to the river 100 miles to the north, the float trip might offer a way to redeem myself and the river.

Finally at noon on the day of departure, after a seemingly interminable time of loading and sweating, fighting mosquitoes and sweating, waiting and sweating, Jim Carrico declared the trip officially begun and pushed the raft out into the current. Seemed a good time to enjoy a celebratory cerveza, since as the rookie on this Rio Grande float trip, I had been assigned the role of observer. Watch and learn, kid.

Carrico, former superintendent at Big Bend National Park and now working for Texas Parks and Wildlife as a west Texas planner and consultant, has spent a good portion of his adult life rafting and canoeing rivers all over the country. He passed out reassurances that he could handle anything that came up. He had the gear. He had the experience. He had the audience. The river was running high, but not dangerously so, and the raft provided a good place from which to sit and soak up some of the most spectacular and still unchanged scenery Mexico and Texas (which used to be Mexico) have to offer.

Texas Parks and Wildlife executive director Andrew Sansom

## DAYS FOURTEEN — SEVENTEEN

*Leaving Rana made going back to being alone really tough. I spent my first night away sleeping on the top of my truck, watching the stars and listening to the Dallas Cowboys on the radio.*

*At dusk, just to complain about the loneliness of the back country where I was camped, I took off all my clothes and ran a mile down the road. Then I ran back. Nobody was there to see. I found an old headstone on a butte miles above the Rio Grande. A young man who died just after World War I, maybe in the flu epidemic. Lonely won't come close to describing what I feel.*

*Stopped to take a picture of a blooming plant and stuck a lechuguilla thorn into the back of my calf. It's still in there and every now and then my leg kind of goes numb. But, the good news is that I've finally hurt myself. It's an official trip.*

*At one place along the river road, I took a trail down to the river. Came up on a bunch of people crossing the river in boats. People on both banks. Don't know what they were doing, but didn't wait to find out. Backed all the way out and hooked it for Rio Grande Village. Had a nice ride on my bike up into the canyon above the river. A roadrunner let me follow him around and take photos. Meeting up with Andy Sansom, Jim Carrico and Dave McNeely was good medicine. We had beer and tacos for lunch in Boquillas to start our trip. I needed the company and beer, and the float trip was hot but good for the soul. We camped one night on the Mexico side. I could hear bats clicking away overhead as they scooped up insects flying over the river. I can hear music coming from the Mexican side of the river. Canyon walls hold heat, so it's a hot night for sleeping. Sansom and I thought we saw a bear so we chased it. Only horses loose in the canyon.*

*I hated to leave my friends, but I can feel the end of this thing coming up. Now I'm driving with a vengeance, headed for the Gulf of Mexico.*

and longtime river runner Dave McNeely were partnered up in a canoe for this trip, a kinship that would offer several attractive photo opportunities as they passed some of the rapids on our three days down the river.

The Rio Grande itself has survived the indignities of channelization and diversion that take place back up toward El Paso, and has begun to cleanse itself through the canyons of the middle Rio Grande. The water is turbid and silty looking, but the bottom is rock and gravel and we took baths each evening with no harmful effect.

I came to see baths in a different light, thinking back especially to the hot springs we'd looked at near Boquillas at the start of our trip. With no running water and no electricity, the citizens of that village use the springs, which flow into the river, as a gathering place, as a laundry and a bathroom. My bath came to be one of the highlights of my day. What a wonderful experience, to sit on a gravel bar like some middle-aged Huck Finn and wash away the sweat and grit from a 100-degree day. Sitting naked in nature's hot tub. Fifteen minutes and youth and energy were restored. I was born again to enjoy a beer and a glass of wine before a Dutch oven dinner.

Ours was an unremarkable trip in terms of danger or tests of boating skills, yet it did open up the Rio Grande for me in several ways. Among them:

* I'd finished the aforementioned river floats, including overnight, without getting in touch with the river itself. Too much emphasis on the thrill aspect of the rapids.

* The Rio Grande has its troubles in some spots, but through the deserts and canyons of west Texas, it remains an untouched resource for recreation, meditation and many other pleasures.

At camp on our second night, Sansom talked about the Rio Grande around Big Bend National Park. "It's majestic," he said. "One of the few places in the state that you could say that about. This is my eighth trip on the river and there's always something unknown." He pointed to bear tracks we'd found on both sides of the river earlier in the day. "When's the last time you saw any bear tracks in Texas?" Sansom asked. "The river is ultimately relaxing, most of all."

That was true. It had even worn away a bit of the edge I felt

ANDREW SANSOM
(LEFT) AND JIM
CARRICO SHARE
LUNCH IN A
SMALL CAFE IN
BOQUILLAS, WHILE
LISTENING TO
A SALES PITCH
FROM A SMALL
BOY SELLING
HANDMADE
BRACELETS.

at not fishing or hunting. Those activities are so much a part of me, so much the way in which I connect with nature, that I find it difficult to enjoy myself outdoors just by being there. I don't have to kill something or catch something and eat it to feel a part of nature, but some piece of my being craves the sense of acting on my instincts for completion. I could feel the others on the trip watching me for my reactions and later they asked if I'd gained enough from our "non-consumptive" trip to want to try it again.

Actually, I had, and I wanted to share it with my wife. I guess that was the missing piece of the puzzle: companionship. Once I had plugged in some people and some good times, I could see float trips for the sake of floating as a part of my life. People are what make them work.

The sweat and physical labor that go into a float trip count too, Sansom said. "A big part of this is an appreciation of the first explorers and settlers in this country. I don't think you can do something like this without a sense of the exploration period. And in Mexico, that's still what it is. This area isn't called La Frontera [The Frontier] for nothing. In my view, a place like this is critical in a state like Texas because there's no place else you can go to get this kind of solitude," Sansom said.

But, despite the isolation, Big Bend and the river still aren't out of reach, Carrico said. "The importance of this place is that it's available as well as accessible to those who are willing to take advantage of it," he said. "You're giving people a chance to test themselves and that just isn't available anywhere else in Texas." The Rio Grande, McNeely added, is always there and rolling along toward the Gulf of Mexico. "It's like life," he said. "It's always moving and changing. You can go over some stretches you've been over before but they still don't look the same."

Let me point out here that the trip didn't dissolve into some drum-thumping, campfire-circling, loincloth-wearing, male-bonding ceremony. It seems to be difficult to separate oneself from the river when you're on it and can't get off, when it now becomes the highway by which you'll get back to civilization.

There is indeed a remarkable appreciation for the accomplishments of the Native Americans and early whites who carved a living out of the region and for the early settlers who mined and ranched here and still do. As we floated along the river, there were constant reminders of the settlers' daring and determination. Rock walls covered the fronts of many caves on bluffs

A FAVORITE SIDELIGHT TO RIO GRANDE FLOAT TRIPS IS SNEAKING UP CANYONS ALONG THE RIVER JUST TO SEE WHAT'S THERE. ONE MIGHT FIND POOLS FOR SWIMMING OR ROCK DRAWINGS OR JUST A DEAD-END CANYON.

VISITORS TO
BOQUILLAS,
MEXICO, CAN BUY A
BOAT RIDE ACROSS
THE RIO GRANDE,
THEN RIDE MULES
UP TO THE VILLAGE.
THE MULES WAIT IN
THE TOWN SQUARE
WHILE TRAVELERS
BUY LUNCH AND
BEER IN NEARBY
CANTINAS.

WITH THE MOUNTAINS
OF MEXICO IN THE
BACKGROUND, ANDREW
SANSOM ROLLS UP HIS
SLEEPING BAG AND
PREPARES FOR ANOTHER
DAY ON THE RIVER.
THIS WAS THE LAST
MORNING OF OUR TRIP.

above the river where some soul had sought shelter and safety from who knows what. And there are signs of mining work and homesites that left me marveling at the labor and determination required just to reach those places at all, much less lug equipment and belongings back there. The people who settled along this river, on both sides, were some tough old bastards.

From time to time, we could hear the squealing of pigs (is there no place they can't live?) from the Mexican side of the river. This was usually accompanied by the sight of a joint of PVC pipe running into the river that would provide some drinking water to a family dwelling back behind the mesquites. The house would be given away by the scent of sewage carried out over the river by the prevailing south winds.

Yet the river, or better said, the land around it, is only nominally changed from what it was 100 or 200 years ago. The desert and the mountains ultimately win on this part of the Rio Grande. This wasn't really meant for human habitation. Nature will allow it for short periods of time, but every once in awhile she sees fit to reestablish the pecking order. Then it's everybody out and start all over.

"You're sitting here and looking out over the landscape and it's the same as when those first sons of bitches came through here," Carrico said. "That's what keeps me here." ■

# THE GOVERNOR

LAJITAS — Air travel and interstate highways have helped change the face of west Texas, even though geography and geology still present formidable fences against worrisome neighbors in the Big Bend.

Change comes slowly to the rugged canyons of the Rio Grande, and it comes not always in the most obvious forms. But it comes. Outside the steep walls of Santa Elena and Mariscal canyons, the real world manifests itself through creeping air pollution, scummy river water and a brand of urban sprawl peculiar to the west Texas desert.

I traveled back to the Rio Grande in west Texas for a springtime float trip with a group headed by Texas governor Ann Richards. It was a combination media moment/campaign trip and vacation to which my presence was somehow considered either a necessary evil or a tolerable intrusion. I could deal with that, even though there was palpable tension the first couple of days until everybody was certain I wasn't going to force career-ending (à la Clayton Williams) quotes out of her.

Richards was a good test on the river, though, because after decades of paddling and drifting her way through the Big Bend region, the governor says she can identify only slight visible alterations in the unique environment of the canyons. The shifts have come from the countries on either side of the river, Richards says, and the only way to retain and restore the character and environment of the region is through the joint efforts of both Texas and Mexico. Richards, who first came to the Rio Grande only at the invitation of friends, said she has special, personal feelings for west Texas. "I'm not a poet," Richards said, "But there is a majesty in these canyons that doesn't exist any other place. There is a quiet that reminds you that the world can be quiet. The closeness of the sky at night is a shock at how many stars there are."

Richards spent four days floating down the Rio Grande, a sort of annual trip with a flotilla of old political allies, friends, family and staff members. Dinner conversation bounced from Washington policy to famous philanderers to problem-solving issues affecting a bi-national wild river.

Even on the Rio Grande, away from big cities and most media, the public and the private Richards are difficult to distinguish. She introduces herself to blue-jeaned youngsters at an eagle release with, "Hi. I'm Ann." The kids were excited about the eagle, but Richards asked about their grades. Autograph seekers, Texans and otherwise, crowd around her on the river bank for photos and quick "we love you" exclamations.

Richards is an interesting study; she comes from that time in Texas when young lawyers left the University of Texas and gravitated toward the legislature and state politics because they believed it was a good thing to do. There are common threads of humor, populism, history and Texas liberalism that run through their conversations, even on a vacation river trip. Raft talk between the governor and her old friends centers on political matters and old times—who seduced whom and passed which bill. She would often take certain individuals, TPWD executive director Andrew Sansom, for instance, into her raft for long discussions.

We approached each other cautiously, I guess. I didn't want to intrude on her vacation, though I did want to talk about the river. She didn't want to let down her guard too much around somebody she knew openly criticized her for removing Chuck Nash as chairman of the Texas Parks and Wildlife Commission, a move that seemed motivated solely by politics and that didn't take into account his service to the state. We nodded and spoke for two days and nights. We both knew some of the same people and sort of communicated through them, until on the third night of our trip, the governor agreed to talk about the Rio Grande. The famous hair in place and a Texas flag flying from a nearby salt cedar, Richards zeroed in on why the river, and experiencing it, are important. "It's not just that this is Texas," Richards said. "There's something about the community of people who run these rivers. The dependency we have on each other to make sure we complete the run. We need the luxury of the drift, to experience the rock formations, the enormous energy it took to create these canyons," she said.

"I love it because there is nothing in the way of modern communications except in an emergency. No phone, no TV, no fax machines, no motors." The isolation, however, only underscores the visible late-twentieth-century intrusions, Richards said, including:

CAMP,
COMPLETE
WITH TEXAS
FLAG, IN
MARISCAL
CANYON.

* Air pollution: This may seem incongruous in a region where the closest large city is 200 miles away, but unregulated emissions in Mexico and increasing human habitation of the desert mean there are many days where the once pristine west Texas sky is hazy and flat. Visibility is less than optimum.

* Water pollution: The Rio Grande suffers from human intervention that occurs hundreds of miles above Big Bend. Even though the waters of Mexico's Rio Conchos (which enters the Rio Grande near Presidio) provide most of the Big Bend flow, water quality remains a problem. There is a scum that forms on the water, Richards said, which is the most visible manifestation of the pollution.

* People: Big Bend is becoming the place to be, and for a region with limited water supplies and a fragile desert ecology, that can mean big problems. Land is for sale, touting new subdivisions, and visitation is increasing annually.

The border itself presents a unique challenge to Mexico and Texas. From El Paso to Brownsville, the countries share the Rio Grande, overlapping cultures and attempts to survive and prosper. "Protection can't be done just in this country," Richards said. "It will take a bi-national agreement."

Texas is nearing completion of an agreement with Mexican governors (slowed by the recent Colosio assassination in Tijuana) that will establish a huge biosphere of protected land on both sides of the Rio Grande as one way the United States and Mexico will be working to preserve the region. "Federal offices dealing with border pollution issues will operate out of El Paso/Juarez," Richards said, "meaning we're not going to have to explain to some bureaucrat what air problems in El Paso mean. Having those offices right here on the border will make all the difference in the world."

Richards said the tough question of limiting access to the river is one facing Texas in the near future. "We've not passed the point of making sure you don't make it worse than it is now," she said, "so you're going to have to limit access and numbers. If it were to become a traffic jam at the Rock Slide [in Santa Elena Canyon] the experience would not be the same. We need to restore our souls and there are not many places where you can do that," Richards said. "I need to be with my friends. This is a very intimate, personal place here. I love it that my daughter is on this trip and that my kids love to run rivers."

"If the river is to remain the thrill it is and have the sort of mystical

**ASSISTANT INTERIOR SECRETARY BOB ARMSTRONG AND SON WILL LEAD A CONTINGENT LEAVING MARISCAL CANYON.**

impact it has on people, it has to continue to be remote, with limited access, strictly enforced," Richards said. "When you stop to think
that more out-of-state visitors came to Big Bend than the Alamo
last year, it gives you some idea of how much this kind of experience means."

The governor and I parted in peace, at least, and credit for that
has to go to the river. Sharing dishwashing duties, bathrooms,
sleeping on the ground and music and talk on dark nights will do
that for people. I guess the governor is right; it is a community. ■

HALLIE STILLWELL HAS
BEEN LIVING IN THE
DESERT ALONG THE
RIO GRANDE SINCE
PANCHO VILLA WAS
RAIDING ACROSS
THE RIVER. SHE IS A
FIXTURE IN WEST
TEXAS, ONE OF THE
TRUE PIONEERS.

# PIONEER SPIRIT

*I've been busy. — Hallie Crawford Stillwell, 1994*

MARATHON — Pancho Villa couldn't chase Hallie Stillwell away from Big Bend and the Rio Grande. Bandits couldn't do it. Drought and sickness and dirt-poor hard times failed, too.

"I never considered leaving," said Stillwell, now 96 years old and a west Texas legend who still lives on the ranch she inherited when husband Roy was killed in 1948. "It wasn't easy, trying to stay alive, but I never wanted to leave. My father said never give up your land. It's the most important thing in life. I've done a lot of things to hold on to the land."

Stillwell has been a rancher and writer, a justice of the peace and an entrepreneur, whatever it took to hold on. Now she holds court at the small store and RV park her family still operates east of Big Bend National Park, showing some visitors through the museum that bears her name or posing for photos and signing copies of her autobiography, *I'll Gather My Geese.*

Each fall Stillwell reigns over a birthday-party/street-dance/hell-of-a-good-time that draws well-wishers from all over the state. They come to pay their respects to the woman who symbolizes the pioneer spirit in Texas.

Hers is a story of optimism and hard work, but to understand it, one must look back nearly a century when Texas was not as old as Stillwell is now and some of the neighboring country hadn't even achieved statehood. "My father homesteaded in New Mexico when it was a territory," Stillwell said. "You had to live on the land three years, then we came back to Alpine to go to school."

Stillwell said her father was a champion of education for his children, though he wasn't prepared for her career choice when she graduated from high school. "I went to Presidio to teach," Stillwell said. "That was during the Pancho Villa days. I had to run from him several times."

When times were good in Presidio, Stillwell and other single teachers shared a small cabin down near the Rio Grande. But when Villa (or sometimes bandits raiding under the auspices of his name) roared into Ojinaga just across the river, the women would have to take shelter inside the Army camp nearby.

The young Hallie Crawford rankled at having to leave her home just because there might be fighting, but remembers what her father had to say about it: "He said, 'Daughter, you're not brave; you just don't have good sense.'"

She likewise didn't care for the attention she received from some of the soldiers in that camp. She was drawn instead toward a rancher from nearby Marathon. Roy Stillwell was from an old, pioneer family, skilled at surviving the rigors of the Big Bend. He held land on both sides of the Rio Grande and was known as something of a rounder.

"I was 20 and he was 40," Stillwell remembers of their 1917 marriage. "I thought it was better to be an old man's darling than a young man's slave." But those might be relative terms when the subject is running a ranch in the Big Bend desert. After their honeymoon, the Stillwells returned to Roy's ranch to begin their married life.

"We had a 12x16 kitchen in the cabin," Stillwell said. That kitchen, which the family has incorporated into the museum, actually was the cabin—and the bedroom and dining room and meeting place. "Roy threw the bedroll on the floor. We'd have to pick it up each morning so the hands could come in for their coffee."

The male-only atmosphere at the ranch had well-established roles wherein all the cleaning, cooking and baking were done by Roy's ranch hands, who made no secret of the fact that they felt bringing a woman to the ranch was a dubious decision. Any violation of the daily protocol—like scrubbing out the coffeepot which had taken years to season—was met with scowls and complaints.

Roy's approach to his wife, and his children when they came along, was trimmed in sink-or-swim colors. Ranch life could be tough, and each person had to find his own way and place. Hallie wasn't to be abused, of course, but she had to learn, much the way a calf had to learn its way around the ranch.

It was during that period of adjustment that the young wife developed the habit of leaving the cooking to the men and finding a place to gather her thoughts. "I usually went outside and sat on a rock," she said. "The hands did the cooking. I didn't do any housework and I'm still not good at it."

But there were other things to do, like working cattle along with Roy and the ranch hands. That was for convenience and safety. "I had to ride with the men because they couldn't leave me alone. There were bandidos, renegades. You had to watch out for them."

Roy stashed a gun in every corner of the small cabin, Stillwell said, with strict orders to shoot any stranger bold enough to violate the ranch rule of coming inside the fence that circled the cabin without an invitation.

Guns were almost as much a way of life as cattle. They meant protection and survival. "I hunted deer whenever we needed food," Stillwell said. "We didn't worry about seasons. I usually shot the deer because I was a better shot than the rest of them."

A few wolves, bears and mountain lions were scattered through the Stillwell ranch country, too. "Once my husband found where a lion had killed a deer," she said. "He told me I could come back in the morning and kill the lion. I was scared. I didn't tell him but I was. Sure enough, I rode up there and I had to get off my horse to shoot him. I thought it was kind of him or me and I shot him right between the eyes."

The hunting instinct has survived, too. Jim Carrico, former superintendent at Big Bend National Park and now supervisor of Big Bend Ranch State Natural Area, tells the story of taking Stillwell on a tour of the ranch after it had been purchased by the state.

"We were driving along when I pointed out a coyote to her," Carrico said with a smile. "All of a sudden she was reaching around behind the seat and all over the car." Carrico realized Stillwell was searching for a rifle to shoot the coyote, the rancher's old nemesis. "I explained that it wasn't legal to do that on the ranch," he said.

Stillwell, who was in her 90s when the coyote incident occurred, admitted to the truth of the story. "That's what coyotes are for," she said.

Action remains the cornerstone of Stillwell's life, optimism the mortar. She bore three children—Son, Dadie and Guy—who remain close. It has been Dadie (Potter) who has driven the work on the Hallie Stillwell Museum as a way of honoring her mother and her life.

"She's been an inspiration," Dadie said. "When something goes wrong, the first thing we think is what would Hallie do. It kind of keeps us going. Her optimism has rubbed off on us and her sense of humor has too."

Roy's death in a truck accident in 1948, the drought of the 1950s, working odd jobs or any jobs just to get by, any one of which might have driven a lesser soul out of the mountains to an easier life in town, have only kept Hallie going. "I'd have thrown up my hands a long time ago, but she always tells us it'll be better tomorrow," Dadie said.

"It takes a certain type of person to live here," Hallie Stillwell said. "The good roads have changed things. Not many people ever came here before the roads were put in. In the old days, when people came, we were really glad to see them." Electricity made its mark in west Texas, but Stillwell said she misses the coal oil lamps she once read by.

Medical care in the first half of the century was rudimentary or nonexistent for ranch dwellers, she said, and the family had to weather some illnesses and cuts and broken bones; but life in the mountains, among the cactus and creosote, was never really scary. There was one time, though. . . .

"I wanted to go down the east side of Stillwell Mountain," Stillwell said. "It's perpendicular. I got halfway down and my horse refused to go any further. I thought I'd die there. Finally, I got behind that horse and pushed him down the mountain. I don't know why I did it, except it was something to be conquered. I wasn't going to rest until I went down that mountain."

But those days are behind her now. Stillwell still clings to the land but she leaves the roughest part of the work to the young folk. She's just concentrating on enjoying her life. She has a plan for the future, too. "I'm 96 years old," she said. "I'm going to live to be past 100 and then I'm going to turn into an old gray mule and I'll be grazing across that hill out there."

Hallie Stillwell was recently inducted into the Texas Women's Hall of Fame. Her autobiography, *I'll Gather My Geese*, is published by Texas A&M University Press. ∎

THE RIO GRANDE AT
THE MOUTH OF
SEMINOLE CANYON
HAS BEGUN TO BE
AFFECTED BY
AMISTAD DAM. THE
RIVER IS AGAIN
CLEAR, CLEAN AND
MIGHTY.

# I WAS HERE

COMSTOCK — Before written history, long before white people boarded horses and trains to settle Texas, bringing their European brand of godliness to the western reaches of the known world, religion already was in full bloom along the Rio Grande.

Native Americans, for whom the river was the center of the universe and survival, used the Rio Grande and its tributaries as travel routes and trading sites. They depended on the food and shelter those valleys and canyons provided. The nomadic lifestyle laid down few literal tracks in the dust, but those early travelers did manage to leave behind a record of their beliefs, some of their culture and their way of life.

One of the best examples of the art of religion can be found in Seminole Canyon State Historical Park, just a stone's throw from the mouth of the Pecos River on the Rio Grande. Much of it done in a unique polychromatic (multicolored) style, the rock art of Seminole Canyon is extensive, clearly defined and open to the public.

"In my mind, the area just west of Langtry down to Amistad Dam and 90 miles north and south of the river, is home to the oldest religious sites in North America," said Solveig Turpin, an anthropologist who has written a book and papers about the region and continues to study the work there. Shamanistic art rendered on the walls of numerous rock shelters in the area, Turpin said, represents the nucleus of a unified belief system. Much of the work depicts shamans in their spirit state carrying out their duties to the society. "It's a figurative death in which he leaves his body and goes to the spirit world to find out why people are sick or where the animals are," Turpin said, pointing out that the beliefs and practices continue in other Native American cultures.

Through work in multiple sites in west Texas, Turpin said, anthropologists have been able to develop an information base

SEMINOLE CANYON IS ONE OF THE FOREMOST ROCK ART FINDS IN THE ENTIRE COUNTRY. NATIVE AMERICANS LIVING HERE FOUND GOOD FOOD AND SHELTER AND OBVIOUSLY TRADED AND TRAVELED IN THE REGION FOR GENERATIONS. THIS DEPICTION IS ONE THAT APPEARS OVER AND OVER AT THE SITE IN SEMINOLE CANYON STATE HISTORICAL AREA.

about many of the figures and what they might mean. And styles changed, too, at least four other times. "We have rock-art sequences of people painting different things to show their interpretation of the world view," she said, "sort of the Kilroy, we-were-here statement."

Rock art continued to some degree, Turpin said. It survived the end of the religion that spawned it, and others came and painted their own messages in the caves. Painting lasted right through the 1870s and "the last gasp of the Plains Indians in Texas." Unfortunately, preservation of the art came much too late to prevent considerable destruction of a number of sites in Texas. Most of that was a lack of information about the significance of the sites, Turpin said, in comparing the Rio Grande rock art to any other religious icons. "The reason I like to put forth the concept of religious art," she said, "is that then most people would see destroying it as an act of desecration."

Turpin said the concept of eco-tourism, taking paying visitors to cultural sites such as Seminole Canyon, is good in terms of heightened awareness, but it runs the risk of elevating the art to commercial status, which could ultimately be harmful. "We have identified more than 1,650 sites in Val Verde County alone, and El Paso County is up over 2,000 sites," Turpin said. "Lots of other counties haven't been looked at yet." The number of sites along the entire reach of the Rio Grande in Texas must number in the tens of thousands, she said.

"Ninety to 95 percent of the shelters have been vandalized," Turpin said. With increased recreational activity in west Texas, the stage is set for problems with keeping the record of habitation intact. "I don't want to see the tourism without the *eco*," she said. Many landowners already are holding firmly to sites on their land, Turpin said, "but much of the land is changing hands and it's a danger. In some places there's a lot of uncontrolled digging." But not all damage is caused by humans, Turpin said. The walls of the caves continually drop pieces of rock. Called ex-foliation, it's a process of aging, of heating and cooling and moisture invasion. Sunlight penetrates some of the caves and when it does, it damages the paintings.

And within those fantastic characters that could come from dreams, and occasional animals being pierced by darts, are many paintings that have been covered by others or by dirt and debris left through centuries of continuous use. They are credited to Archaic Indians, who lived in the region 2,000–12,000 years ago, but the historic tribes in the region were Apaches. Despite what many people believe about the rock art along the Rio Grande, Turpin says the drawings do not depict hunting scenes, though the people using the area certainly did hunt. "The animals [in the art] are probably familiars, shapes the shamans could assume," Turpin said.

"What's really important about this is it's the only place in Texas where you have the world view of these people painted on the walls," she said. "No other people in Texas did it or it didn't survive if they did." The paintings show an elaborate supernatural world, Turpin said, but not one without structure." Certain figures are found in multiple places," she said. That's similar to finding crucifixes in Catholic churches, for instance, and indicates that the people moved around and carried with them their beliefs and cultural values.

"These big sites are where people came together to exchange news, find husbands and wives, all kinds of cultural and economic exchanges," Turpin said. Even the most special locations were probably occupied only on a cyclical basis and by whoever traveled through, but there is evidence some people may have laid greater claims than others. In Panther Cave, for instance, there are nine different versions of cats and panthers painted on the walls, Turpin said. "They were plainly saying we're the Panther People. This is our place." Whether that meant any violent competition for the shelter, or just that someone might have to move on if the Panther People came back, no one knows.

And that may ultimately be the most important thing about rock art, which appears in varying forms throughout the entire stretch of the Rio Grande: Nobody knows. We draw conclusions, of course, based on things we do know and are able to deduce through study; but the very basic act—the state of mind of that artist, the bend of his mind—we do not, *can* not know.

Maybe on that day religious ardor poured over him in the form of a mighty south Texas thunderstorm. Or a spike of hunger drove him to cry out to some higher power for help in finding animals to hunt. Or maybe he was just bored and decided to copy the drawings of an unknown fellow traveler. Or just maybe, in the case of the Panther People, he was leaving his gang's scrawl on that rock because there were no phone booths, junction boxes or brick walls to mark territorial boundaries in those days.

## DAY EIGHTEEN

*Spent one night at Seminole Canyon and another in Del Rio getting some work done. Ran in the desert and it was spectacular. The air smells like honey. There are quail and deer and snakes and it's a wonderful place to be. Have found that I'm getting used to sleeping on the ground and get more rest outside than in a motel. Feel like I'm missing big parts of the Rio Grande and south Texas, though, as I'm coming down. But gravity has taken over and I'm headed on to the coast. Can come back again to fill in gaps. Got caught in traffic at international bridge in Laredo and sent over into Nuevo Laredo. Trolled around a while and went back. Customs agent wondered about all the stuff in the truck and made me unload and explain.*

And there is in that thought some comfort for the less mystical, gimme-cap side of me. To think that some ancient soul just did it, wrote a few words or drew a stick man for the hell of it. I've hunted through aspen groves in Colorado and Wyoming and in certain places—mountain passes, along stream beds, obvious campsites—people have carved names and initials and dates into the trees. Some mark nothing more consequential than a campsite, others that a deer or elk died in this spot. A few, though, note with two pairs of initials that a couple chose to pledge their love in this arbor. (One even graphically detailed the sex that went with that pledge.)

I would like to think that those Apaches had something in common with us in the twentieth century, even if the band that stretches between our days on earth is nothing more than an interest in graffiti. But it's really more than graffiti, I think. It's one man's, one people's way of saying, "I was here. I tried to make some sense of it all. I did the best I could. I wrote some of it down and then I moved on."

Your turn. ■

I DIDN'T THINK TOO MUCH ABOUT THIS DRILLING SITE IN FALCON LAKE STATE PARK WHEN IT WAS APPROVED BY THE TEXAS PARKS AND WILDLIFE DEPARTMENT. SEEING IT UP CLOSE AND PERSONAL WAS AN UGLY, EYE-OPENING, SLEEP-ROBBING EXPERIENCE.

THE TEXAS TORTOISE
ISN'T AN ENDANGERED
SPECIES, BUT THE
DETERMINED LITTLE
BEASTS, SO IMPORTANT
TO THE ECOLOGY OF
THE SOUTH TEXAS
DESERT, ARE THRE
ATENED BY TRUCKS
AND CARS ON THE
ROADS IN AND
AROUND THE PARK.

# TORTOISES AND GAS WELLS

**F**ALCON HEIGHTS — Tortoises are tough.
Tortoises are stubborn, and tortoises are quick, in their own way. Tortoises cannot, in any way, on any day, win a game of one-on-one with an 18-wheeler.

If this one wasn't going to wind up critter du jour, a greasy spot on a 52-inch wheel, he was going to need some help getting across the entrance road to Falcon Lake State Park. I stopped my truck and snatched him out of the way of one of the drilling rig trucks that are constantly going in and out of the park. Suddenly, the state-approved gas well drilling that's going on in the park, which I'd written about but never seen, took on a whole new shade of ugly. I'd listened to it and endured the lights going the whole night before, but this tortoise put a new face on what was happening.

Animals, of course, don't have the same emotions humans do. But this tortoise, a Texas tortoise, had an elegant and reserved air about him that was so much more attractive than a gas truck could ever be. I had to wonder how many of them, along with a variety of snakes, snails, birds and other critters had wound up in the classic armadillo pose, feet up and eyes closed, on the yellow strip. And beyond that, I wondered about the tortoise. What was he and what was his story? The man with all the answers, the tortoise rabbi himself, turned out to live back in central Texas, Southwest Texas State University biology professor Francis Rose.

It seems that the Texas tortoise, one of four species found in the southern United States, is a critical member of the southwestern desert culture. It all starts with his diet. Quick or not, he can't go out and catch food, so obviously he depends on something standing still. "They really like those red tunas [bulbs] off prickly pear," Rose said. "And we've found the seeds pass through the tortoise and the pear grows better." Then all sorts of critters live in and around the prickly pear, including

## DAY NINETEEN

Waded around some hydrilla on Falcon Reservoir and caught a couple of bass with my fly rod. The lake was teeming with fish, but not many people in my camping area. Also think I'm getting weird from being alone so much. Emotional. On the verge of becoming a card-carrying, bunny-hugging, fern-kissing, save-the-river maniac. Or just a maniac. Ran after dark and tripped over a speed bump. Looks like I lost a fight with Tyson.

wood rats. Snakes, lizards and even tortoises find winter shelter in the middens the rats construct beneath the cactus.

"We've also found that if you kill off the rattlesnake population in an area, the wood rats increase and they'll eat the live tortoise shells in the winter. So you need the rats, the tortoises and the snakes in the prickly pear. That cactus community is very complex."

Rose has been studying the Texas tortoise for 30 years. During that time, he's developed quite a fondness for the little critters, which are usually eight to 10 inches high, maybe slightly longer if a male. Rose's affinity for tortoises pales by comparison to some, though. "We've found some that have been passed along in wills in south Texas," he said. "People just collect them as youngsters and get attached to them. That's how we know that some of them are more than 70 years old. They've been held for that long."

The tortoises are protected, Rose said, so technically they can't be held in captivity, but with the multi-generational pets the state usually looks the other way. Some of those older animals offer information and background, though. Rose will take those wherever he can get them. "We really know very little about them, though they're the only tortoise that occurs in numbers big enough to be studied." Those numbers have declined over the years and Rose really can't say why. He speculates that he may have begun his study in a couple of places when the population was abnormally high and that low densities are really the norm. "There's been a steady decline, but it's in places where the habitat has declined so we don't know. We're going to try to find out."

Rose has already begun extensive radio telemetry work on tagged tortoises on the Chaparral Wildlife Management Area in south Texas and hopes to expand that to other areas. "Their range runs roughly from the east coast of Mexico, up through Del Rio, south to San Antonio and on over to the coast." Tortoises seem to have a home range, Rose said, but they do funny things at times. "We would find an animal over and over in one area, then they would disperse for two years and then come back," he said. That could just be a weird thing they do, or it could be they haven't been found at other times on their travels, or it could mean nothing.

"They don't fight for territory, we know," he said. "But they fight like little tanks. They'll fight sometimes for hours." That's usually over a female. Occasionally one will be flipped over onto his back and be unable to right himself, Rose said. The sentence, of course, is death.

The tortoise's main diet is vegetarian, and he is a cropper, meaning he eats whatever he passes that passes the taste test. Females during egg-laying times will eat snails, possibly for the calcium for constructing egg shells, Rose said.

Males along the Gulf Coast seem to be much bigger than their counterparts inland, but either way they are built for power and durability. Their shells are heavy and thick. There is a horn that sticks out in front on the bottom. They use that to ram opponents in fights. And as I said, they're pretty quick on their feet. The specimen I picked up sulked for a few minutes until he was certain I wasn't going to try to eat him or something. Then he just seemed to poke out his head and legs, dust himself off, and depart. Back across the highway. ■

A CHACHALACA IN
BENTSEN-RIO GRANDE
STATE PARK, ONE
OF THE FOREMOST
BIRD-WATCHING
AREAS IN THE
COUNTRY. ON A
LATE-AFTERNOON JOG
IN THE PARK, I SAW A
JAGUARUNDI DART
OUT OF THE JUNGLE
FOR A MOMENT.

# CATS AND OTHER CATS

**M**cALLEN — They call them charismatic mega-fauna—ocelots and jaguarundis—the high-profile endangered species which carry the banner for all of south Texas in the battle for federal funding for habitat preservation and restoration.

They've come a long way over the years. The federal government has more than 63,000 acres of land under management, with an ultimate goal of 132,000. The Lower Rio Grande Valley Wildlife Refuge, also known as the Wildlife Corridor, is an all-out effort to stop degradation of land and water along the river.

The Lower Rio Grande Valley has been forever changed, of course, much like the rest of the river, by agriculture and development. The resulting loss of habitat knocked big holes in the populations of ocelots and jaguarundis, small wildcats that live in south Texas and Mexico. Ocelots are spotted cats of 20–35 pounds, with long tails. Jaguarundis are dark in color, with short legs and a long, thick tail. Both are mostly nocturnal and difficult to study.

While suitable habitat still exists, it is fractured and the corridor concept is seen as a way to allow the animals to disperse at adulthood and move to populate new areas. A major loss of ocelots has always occurred on highways as maturing animals seek suitable locations to establish a new home. "The idea behind the corridor is to link up these pieces of habitat," said Mike Bryant, refuge manager in McAllen. "Isolation is a danger because you can have inbreeding and disease." The habitat is essential to the survival of the cats, but more than 100 species have been identified as relying on the same habitat. Some plants in the region are down to a single individual plant.

It is a dark time for the Lower Valley, but also one of hope for saving some parts of it. Inside the war rooms of conservation agencies, Bryant said, the talk is not necessarily of specific cats. He admitted, though, that they make nice symbols for marshaling support and helping raise money. Funds come from the Land and Water Conservation Fund, which has pumped more than $60 million into the valley already.

THIS ROADRUNNER
KEPT ME BUSY FOR A
COUPLE OF HOURS AT
MY CAMP ON THE RIO
GRANDE. HE HAD
BECOME ACCUSTOMED
TO PEOPLE AND DIDN'T
MIND LETTING ME TAG
ALONG WHILE HE
HUNTED LIZARDS.

The Rio Grande has some interesting characteristics in the Lower Valley. It is the only water source. No tributaries flow into the river from Falcon Dam all the way to Boca Chica. The river actually is the highest point in the Valley and all water that can escape the river bank flows away from it. It's not unusual, then, that the riparian habitat hosts so many endangered species. Nothing can exist without the Rio Grande.

In building the refuge system, which runs basically from Falcon Dam to the mouth of the river, the federal government and private partners have begun the process of reversing habitat loss. "We have some areas that are getting close to meeting our requirements," Bryant said. "The migratory birds that come through here are doing pretty well, for instance, but certain birds that nest here have greater needs."

Threatened and endangered plants are another matter. Walker's manioc is one of those plants with just one individual remaining. They are in big trouble. One flood, one parasite, bad weather could wipe them out.

Gary Waggerman, a wildlife biologist for Texas Parks and Wildlife, has been involved in the state agency's restoration and acquisition programs in the Lower Rio Grande Valley since 1978. The state now has 19 sites, mostly purchased with white-winged dove stamp funds, scattered up and down the river. "We want to help all the critters that exist and would have if the farm land hadn't been there," Waggerman said. "Restoration is a big part of what we do and we're also working on restoring private lands. It's going a lot faster than I thought it would." Waggerman said native habitat is at a high mark right now with more to come as the state and federal governments gain funding for their projects.

But one need only drive through the area to see the utter devastation wreaked by the clearing of land for agriculture and human dwellings. The brush that once ran many miles inland now is restricted to small strips along the river and the various sites held by governmental agencies. It's a demoralizing drive, actually.

Bryant, though, is hopeful and determined that the valley be restored for the benefit of the plants and animals, as well as the people. "If we just wanted to see an ocelot, we could go to a zoo. If we get into the environment where they live, we're going to see other animals. We need 250,000 total acres to protect the wildlife."

The Rio Grande is central to that effort. If it's degraded or drained, the wildlife suffer. Bryant believes it's now or never. "The clock is ticking on some of the wildlife." ∎

### DAY TWENTY

Rolled into McAllen early this morning from Falcon. Along the way, passed a shop with a sign that said, "Chacho's Auto Salvage and Video Center." Now that I'm in the Lower Valley, some things are certain: Church's Fried Chicken in every town and a garage sale in every yard. Ate chicken again in Rio Grande City or some place like that. Got sick again.

### DAY TWENTY-ONE

Spent the night in Bentsen–Rio Grande State Park, one of the premier bird-watching areas in Texas. Mostly by myself, but there was one family barbecue going on. Ran through the park at dusk and actually saw a jaguarundi. May have seen an ocelot, but too far away and too dark to be sure. Could have been a bobcat.

# REDFISH AT SUNUP

FISHING GUIDE
STEVE ELLIS
ADMIRES A
REDFISH
CAUGHT ON A
FLY ROD NEAR
THE MOUTH OF
THE RIVER.

SOUTH PADRE ISLAND — Just enough chill hung on the air to force me into a windbreaker on the ride across the lagoon to the south shore of Laguna Atascosa National Wildlife Refuge. Steve Ellis steered a strict course and the flat-bottomed boat skimmed effortlessly over the shallow water.

A tiny chop blown by a light southeast wind set up a rhythm on the bottom of the boat and it was easy to slip into a kind of trance, feeling the wind in my face and the hum of the water coming up through the wide front seat. There was a mild irritation when Ellis cut the engine and let the boat glide to a stop, not unlike the vague emptiness that comes with being torn away from a particularly nice dream; but stopping let heat from the rising sun soak in and that felt nice.

"We'll just move around here on this shoreline, looking for redfish feeding against the grass," Ellis said as he mounted the poling platform at the rear of the boat. "Everything is perfect. We'll find some fish." I climbed into casting position on the front tower feeling just slightly outgunned with the light 7-weight fly rod. Redfish, technically red drum, are the mules of saltwater game fish, strong fighters capable of long battles and in late summer, lengths and weights that can put pressure on much heavier tackle.

Ellis, though, is one of a small group of fishing guides operating now on the lower Texas coast who cater solely to fly fishermen. He and I had fished together in the past and I knew I could count on him to get me into position at least to hook a redfish. "I love fly fishermen and fly fishing," Ellis said. "It's much more like hunting because we are casting to particular fish. And we release everything we catch. I don't allow anybody to keep fish anymore and fly fishermen don't care."

After more than three weeks on the road, worrying about things other than fishing, I didn't start out with my head in the game. Ellis spotted one fish tailing along the island shore, but I

**SUNRISE
FISHING
AT SOUTH
PADRE
ISLAND.**

never really got the fly in the right position. At the third cast, the redfish exploded away in a flash of bronze. "That's okay," he said. "I see one right over here that we're going to catch. Look, right at the sun, he's halfway out of the water. He's ours."

Our redfish was indeed halfway out of the water. So intent was he on the shrimp and crabs he was scooping up that Ellis was able to maneuver the boat to within 30 feet. I made one bad cast, stripped the streamer back and shot another cast in front of and 10 feet past the moving fish. "That's perfect!" Ellis exclaimed from behind me. "Watch his fins flare." Caudal and anal fins flared a bright orange as the redfish torpedoed forward and the streamer disappeared. I could see it all from almost directly overhead. I leaned back on the rod and the big red, nearly 29 inches long, shot across the flat into slightly deeper water where he'd have more fighting leverage. But with the long rod and high angle, even that was useless. I landed him at least as fast as I could have with casting tackle.

"Look at the spots!" Ellis said, admiring a fish that sported 10 distinct spots on either side instead of the customary one or two. It was the most beautiful redfish I'd ever seen and having caught him on a fly rod seemed somehow right with the world here at the end of the Rio Grande. Amazingly, we would be able to repeat the scenario half a dozen times more before noon on the most perfect fishing day I've ever experienced.

Some fishing trips, whether because of the quality of the company or just the mood I'm in that day, demand that I never let up on the fish. If they'll bite, I'll fish for them. Other days, the end comes sooner but with no less a feeling of completion. After the seventh fish, all hooked on attacking strikes, had been landed, photographed and released, Ellis suggested another area to better deal with a building southerly breeze.

I could catch more fish, but I couldn't make this a better day than it already was. Home, family were waiting six hours up the road. "Let's call it a day," I said, almost to myself. "Let's go home." ∎

## DAY TWENTY-TWO

*I can't take any more. I'm going to push it to the end of the river, fish for a day and split. I'll come back and do this again. It will be tough, though, to go back to civilization, where I have to pee in a toilet and take baths every day. I'm tired of this damned diary, though, and tired of watching other people with their spouses and kids. I want to go home. Signing off.*

# BACK HOME AGAIN

BOCA CHICA — I feel like I could reach across and touch Mexico right now. I'm standing ankle deep in the surf at the mouth of the Rio Grande, watching a Mexican family fishing on their side of the river. I'm rolling Country and Western songs over in my mind.

John Denver, "Back Home Again." Johnny Rodriguez, "Down on the Rio Grande." Somebody I can't remember, "Just Call Me Lonesome." I'm getting ready to go home and the little domestic scene on the sand spit across the way stirs something pretty deep inside me. Real men may not, but I'd eat quiche and ladyfingers to be home right now.

Boca Chica is a place, not a city. It means "little mouth"—an apt appellation. I came down here originally to wade out and fish for the snook that are supposed to be working the rip at the mouth of the Rio Grande. To get these 10 miles from my motel, I drove clean back into Brownsville and over to Boca Chica, an hour-long excursion. Once I hit the beach, though, and headed west toward the river, I knew I wouldn't fish. I pulled a beer out of the ice chest and sat and watched the surf fishermen on both sides. They weren't catching many fish and I didn't want to get wet anyway.

Brown pelicans, once endangered but now easy to find on the coast, glide along parallel to the third bar. I can't tell if they are fishing or just heading for their nighttime perch. Laughing gulls, skimmers and kildeers work the shallow water and the beach, keeping a respectful distance but not paying much attention to me. This would be a good placc to pitch a sleeping bag, but frankly, it doesn't feel all that safe trapped up against the river. I decide to wait an appropriate length of time (so it won't appear that I'm afraid and running away from the mostly Hispanic beach crowd) and then pack up my cameras and head back to the motel.

Then I spent a miserable night trying to sleep on a lousy

A MEXICAN FAMILY
FISHES IN THE SURF
AT THE MOUTH OF
THE RIVER. HERE AT
THE GULF OF MEXICO,
THE RIVER AGAIN IS
SHALLOW AND WIDE.

motel bed that sagged in the middle and rocked endlessly each time I rolled over. Definitely time to go home. I was at the end of a trip that had taken nearly a month, and by the time I got back to the Hill Country the next day I would have logged more than 4,500 miles on the truck odometer. This was a really spooky time for me, one that I always have at the end of an assignment but that came in waves down here. I had exposed rolls and rolls of film, but were the photos any good? I had some interviews that interested me, but trying to cram 2,000 miles of river and 150 years of history and stories into a small space seemed beyond my limited capabilities.

I could look back up the river from its source and see in my mind the place where it all began, a nondescript bit of snow and ice far up in the mountains of Colorado. I had traveled more than one river, though all were tagged with the name Rio Grande. They flowed in one continuous bed, too, but geography and politics demanded that certain stretches change to meet human needs. Rarely did humans change to accommodate the river, though that did happen some with the river runners and with the Indians I passed along the way.

The Rio Grande—historic, vital, polluted. It seems gratuitous to say that I vowed down there to find out more, but I did. I want to travel on the Rio Grande again, to look for other rivers I've yet to discover. It was the end of a trip, but the river goes on.

In the words of Mark Twain, there is the story, most of it is true. ∎

# INDEX